italia

...

alex ramsay and helena attlee

italian gardens

● ● ● ellipsis

•••

BRITISH LIBRARY CATALOGUING IN PUBLICATION
A CIP record for this book is available from the British Library

PUBLISHED BY •••ellipsis
2 Rufus Street London N1 6PE
EMAIL ...@ellipsis.co.uk
www http://www.ellipsis.com

COPYRIGHT © 2000 Alex Ramsey and Helena Attlee

DESIGN Jonathan Moberly
LAYOUT Mark Wilson

Printed in Hong Kong

ISBN 1 899858 53 9

•••ellipsis is a trademark of Ellipsis London Limited

For a copy of the Ellipsis catalogue or information on special
quantity orders of Ellipsis books please contact Faye Chang on
020 7739 3157 or faye@ellipsis.co.uk

contents

introduction

For centuries travellers have been drawn to the gardens of Italy, and their admiring and astonished comments fill the pages of countless letters and diaries. Anyone willing to leave the well-trodden paths of tourism to seek the lesser-known gardens included here will find them still compellingly beautiful. The dark green of cypress and yew, black shadows, pale statues and shimmering pools leave lasting impressions on the imagination.

Before its unification in 1860, Italy was divided into numerous independent states, which until the seventeenth century were often at war with one another. This turbulent history meant that conditions were not always propitious to the cultivation of gardens. However, peace and prosperity did visit the different regions of Italy at different times, a fact reflected in the creation of new gardens and the extension of old ones.

The Italian climate and landscape vary enormously from one end of the country to the other. In the north, with its high rainfall and relatively level terrain, gardens were not only easy to create, but also easy to alter as fashion succeeded fashion. In the south, however, water shortage, poverty and constant political turmoil have meant that few gardens of note survive.

Very few medieval gardens survive in Italy. However, there is ample written evidence throughout Europe to give an indication of what they were like. Pleasure gardens were generally small, enclosed areas laid down to grass, with a central pool. The surrounding wall might have been covered with climbers, such as honeysuckle, or with grapevine.

These simple meads were very different from the splendid pleasure-gardens created in Sicily after the ninth-century Arab conquest. They were all destroyed during the Norman invasion of 1091 but were probably similar to the Moorish gardens still found in Spain. The Arabs, however, did leave one major legacy, for it was they who first imported the ubiquitous orange and lemon trees. The Normans in their turn made gardens in the Moorish style, though few survive (Villa Rufolo in Ravello is a rare exception).

The great gift that Italian garden designers have given the rest of Europe is their reinterpretation of the classical traditions of the ancient world. Generally, many ancient Greek and Roman literary works were known in the Middle Ages, but there was especial interest in the culture of the classical world at the beginning of the fifteenth century. This was a contributing factor to the rise of humanism, the key that unlocked the energies of the period now called the Renaissance.

The turning point of these early years was the publication of *De re Aedificatoria* (1452, published 1485) by the Florentine architect and humanist Leon Battista Alberti. He looked to the classical authors of ancient Rome for inspiration, his principal sources being Vitruvius' *De Architectura*, the sole-surviving architectural treatise from antiquity (first century BC), and the letters of the lawyer/administrator Pliny the Younger, written in the first century AD and giving an idea of privileged life in his villas in the country at Tusculum and by the sea at Laurentum. Alberti's reinterpretation of the classical traditions of the ancient world was to determine the form taken by the early Renaissance gardens of Tuscany. He was not concerned so much with their layout as with their situation. Following Pliny's lead, hillside sites were preferred on account of the sun, the cool breeze and the view. The view should overlook 'the city, the owner's land, the sea or a great plain and familiar hills and mountains', while in the foreground 'there should be the delicacy of gardens'. An early Tuscan garden built a few years later at the Palazzo Piccolomini in Pienza, a town in parts remodelled in accord with Alberti's architectural theories, displays this vision to perfection. Gardens of the early Renaissance were designed with the utmost simplicity, the space often divided by hedges into a series of enclosures or 'garden rooms'.

Alberti's influence extended beyond the boundaries of the Florentine Republic. In the early years of the sixteenth century leadership in garden design passed from Tuscany to Rome, and it was here, with the patronage of the great princes of the Church, that the Classical Renaissance style developed. Like Alberti's treatise, the new Roman style was dependent on two antiquarian influences, namely the adoption of ancient styles gleaned from archaeological investigation and close interpretation of literary descriptions. For example, Donato Bramante's Cortile del Belvedere at the Vatican (1504) exploited the landscape with terraces and impressive flights of steps, tunnels and galleries, in emulation of the scale and massing of the Temple of Fortuna Primigenia at Palestrina (c. 80 BC), while Raphael's Villa Madama, just outside Rome (begun 1517), had the scale and layout of imperial baths while incorporating the Plinian sentiments of life in a country villa. The gardens they made to complement these architectural displays of wealth and power were quite different from the modest designs of the early Renaissance. So too was their use of statuary as essential elements, again based on descriptions of their disposition in Greek and Roman gardens or public spaces. (Alberti had unwillingly conceded their occasional use 'if not indecent'!)

The gardens of the Renaissance reflected a secure and ordered world picture. Towards the mid-sixteenth century, however, a sense of insecurity began to pervade the arts. It is said that it began with the bar-

baric violence of the Sack of Rome in 1527, a thrust at the very heart of the civilised world. The Mannerist style that developed around this time changed gardens from havens of peace and repose to places of discovery and entertainment, filled with water-powered automata and *giochi d'acqua*, or 'water tricks', the latter being water jets concealed throughout the garden. Only the owner (and perhaps his staff) knew where to find the controls, and this allowed him to soak his unlucky guests to the skin at will. The second development was the appearance of the 'iconographic' garden. By using the ornamentation and layout of a garden to refer to the then widely known events of classical mythology, a range of philosophical ideals could be expressed and, if so wished, could flatter the owner or his guests. The fullest expression of both these developments is at the Villa d'Este at Tivoli, itself situated close to Hadrian's Villa (AD 118–25), probably the greatest imperial palace and garden complex of the Roman Empire.

Until the beginning of the seventeenth century the natural landscape had no place within the boundaries of the garden. Even the 'wild' aspect of the bosco owed more to artistry than nature. However, the fluid forms that typify the Baroque in art found their expression in garden design in a new relationship with the landscape. The boundaries between art and nature became less distinct. The garden might merge into the encroaching forest (as it does at the Villa Aldobrandini at Frascati) or it might be completely dominated by the surrounding landscape (as at Cetinale near Siena). The most distinctive Baroque garden of all is Isola Bella on Lago Maggiore, at the feet of the Alps on the Italian lakes, with an architectural style that is both flamboyant and in perfect harmony with its surroundings.

By the mid-eighteenth century Italian garden design had lost much of its vitality. The formal French style, as typified by André Le Nôtre's garden at Versailles outside Paris, had been adopted in many gardens in northern Italy; and by the beginning of the nineteenth century the fashion for the English landscape garden spread across Italy, supplanting countless formal gardens whose unrecorded beauty is lost to us for ever.

ARTISTS AND WRITERS

Contemporary prints, engravings and descriptions are a valuable source of information about the original design of gardens and their subsequent history. And indeed it was these very engravings coupled with the experiences and accounts of travellers on the Grand Tour that ensured the spread of classicism in general and the Italian Renaissance garden in particular throughout Europe. Certain names will recur frequently in the text, though to avoid repetition the main players will be outlined here.

Giovanni Battista Falda engraved the great villas and monuments of Rome during the seventeenth century; Giuseppe Zocchi performed much the same task in Tuscany during the eighteenth century; while the Austrian J C Volkamer published engravings of all the great gardens of the Veneto, and of specimens of the citrus fruit cultivated there. Marcantonio dal Re's book of prints and descriptions of the villas in Lombardy was also published in the eighteenth century.

Another valuable source of information is in the diaries of contemporary travellers. Those of John Evelyn, the seventeenth-century English diarist and garden writer who travelled in Italy, have been referred to continuously. Also, the letters of President de Brosses, a French magistrate who travelled the length and breadth of the country during the eighteenth century, have been drawn on.

At the beginning of this century the gardens of Italy were 'rediscovered' by foreign visitors. One of the most perceptive was the American author Edith Wharton, whose subtle and detailed analyses of individual gardens are as valid today as they were when her *Italian Villas and their Gardens* was published in 1904. Also included are some magnificent garden plans by the English architect and garden designer Harry Inigo Triggs, first published in 1906. Among many subsequent publications Georgina Masson's beautifully photographed *Italian Gardens* (1961) introduced the general public to the Italian garden, and her learned, intimate and enthusiastic analysis of the gardens she rediscovered and researched was welcome and timely. Most recently, and especially in the past 10 years, there has been a rise in studies of the Italian garden generally, which in Italy has coincided with the setting up of the FAI (Fondo per l'Ambiente Italiano), an organisation that fulfils much the same role as The National Trust does in Britain. The FAI has attracted a wide membership and has begun to assist in the management of certain gardens. Fortunately, many private owners and public administrators recognise the unique value and vulnerability of the gardens in their care, and they are both willing and able to meet the ever increasing costs of maintaining them.

Our research has taken us to the sites of several famous gardens that have been completely destroyed by urban development, neglect and vandalism. Despite their historic importance, they hardly merit a visit by even the most dedicated enthusiast. A poignant example is Andrea Doria's garden, which once covered the hillside above the Bay of Genoa. It has been replaced by an open-air cinema and a motorway flyover. Another is Villa Venaria Reale, which was originally the most spectacular of Turin's seventeenth-century gardens. It is now derelict. The famous garden of Pratolino (Parco Demidoff) near Florence met with a different form of destruction. The Austrian Duke Ferdinand objected to the cost of its upkeep and had it replaced by an English landscape garden in 1819. Fortunately things have changed, and it is good to know that national concern for garden conservation is higher now than at any time this century. We hope that this book will encourage visitors to go to the gardens of Italy in increasing numbers and will help to swell the growing tide in favour of conservation and restoration.

ACKNOWLEDGEMENTS
Our gratitude and thanks are due to all the garden owners and gardeners whose loving labours have created and preserved the gardens of Italy. So many have been helpful that they cannot all be mentioned. Our thanks to them all, most particularly for their generosity in making the gardens accessible to visitors. Many public officials and organisations were most generous with time and information. Among them, we thank: Dr Renata Lodari (Consigliere del Museo di Verbania), Dr Paolo Odone (Direttore Servizio Giardini, Turin), Drs Pellizon and Zago (Regione del Veneto), Dr Giancarlo della Santa (Segretario Regionale 'Agriturist', Florence), and the staff of the Ente di Turismo, Salerno.

Thanks, too, to the authorities at the Quirinal gardens in Rome for their interest and assistance. Our labours were considerably lightened by the support and encouragement of our friends, especially those with whom we stayed on our many journeys. Much as we would like to, we cannot mention them all, but especial thanks to: Luigina Benci, Sulie and François Bruzzi, Stefanella Griccioli, Anne and Giovanni Grotanelli, Piera and Annibale Osti, and last but not least to Valeria Grilli, whose kindness to us and to our riotous one-year-old daughter rose far above the call of friendship.

In general, the optimum times for garden visiting are from mid-April to mid-June and from the beginning of September to mid-October. Some garden owners prefer visitors to make an appointment, which usually can be done by telephone. Also, it is suggested that you approach the local tourist office (*azienda di soggiorno*) or your hotel for help.

Good maps are essential. The TCI (Touring Club Italiano) 1:200,000 series, in the green covers, is recommended – it is inexpensive and widely available.

Provisions for visitors should not be expected: many of the gardens are privately owned and refreshments or lavatories will probably not be provided. However, we have indicated where facilities are available. Also, many gardens are on steep slopes and provision is rarely made for wheelchairs. Again, those gardens better suited to wheelchair users are indicated in the text.

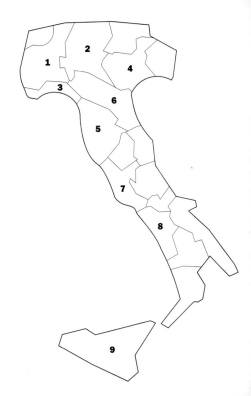

1 piedmont
2 lombardy
3 liguria
4 veneto
5 tuscany
6 emilia romagna
7 lazio
8 campania
9 sicily

piedmont

regional introduction

Piedmont is the northernmost region of Italy, running from the Alps to the flat plains around the river Po. The winters can be severe, though Lago Maggiore has its own mild microclimate.

The region has had a close relationship with France since the eleventh century, when the ruling house of Savoy gained possession of Turin. This is reflected in the design of some of its most important gardens. When in 1697 Vittorio Amadeo II wanted to create a new garden for the ducal palace, he turned to the French garden designer André Le Nôtre for help. Similarly in 1740 Carlo Emanuele called in the French father-and-son architects, the Bernards, to lay out the garden of his new 'hunting box' – actually the magnificent palace of Stupinigi. Even Italian garden architects working in Piedmont had a tendency to adopt the details of French design. Green wooden boxes replaced terracotta pots for lemons, and the deciduous trees that grow so well in the region were planted in avenues in the French manner.

The gardens of Villa Regina and Venaria Reale, once well known for their scale and beauty, have been allowed to decay to such an extent that they no longer merit inclusion in a guidebook, though it is still possible to visit them.

NEAREST MAJOR TOWN Turin
MAIN FEATURES vast seventeenth-century palace with seventeenth- and eighteenth-century garden and park in a rural setting
PRE-BOOKING no
OWNER the State
ADDRESS Piazza del Castello, I-1001I Agliè

LOCATION follow signs for the A5 to Aosta from the centre of Turin. Agliè is 33 kilometres north of the city
OPEN Thursday to Sunday 9.00–12.00, 14.00–18.00
ADMISSION L4000; free for children and adults more than 60 years old
WHEELCHAIRS no
REFRESHMENTS no
LAVATORIES yes

The Castello di Agliè was built for the San Martino d'Agliè in the early seventeenth century. The names of the architect and garden designer are not recorded. The palace and grounds are depicted in the inventory of the possessions of the House of Savoy known as the *Theatrum Sabaudiae* of 1682. Unfortunately the accuracy of these prints can not be relied on. It was not mere artistic licence that led the artists to exaggerate the size and splendour of the buildings and gardens. Their imaginations were fired by the need to produce images that would glorify the Duchy of Savoy. However, Agliè is immediately recognisable. The vast mass of the building rises up from a terrace decorated with pots of lemon. The accuracy of many aspects of this print can be confirmed by the layout of the gardens today. At this time it was the home of Filippo d'Agliè, gentleman-in-waiting to the Duke of Savoy, Master of the Armoury, Minister of Finance, poet, writer and a great favourite at court.

In 1764, Agliè was bought by Carlo Emanuele II for his son Benedetto Maurizio, Duke of Chablis. Alterations were made to the palace and garden. During the Napoleonic occupation the park was separated from the rest of the property and bought by a lawyer called Genta. In the nineteenth century it returned to the House of Savoy and was finally bought by the State in 1939.

The magnificent façade of the palace overlooks a wide terrace lined with lemons in faded green boxes. The arcaded entrance, which is linked to the piano nobile by a grand staircase, creates a shady extension to the terrace.

Below the terrace is the English garden, reached by a double set of balustraded steps. The garden consists of a circular pool surrounded by a lawn and bounded by trees on two sides. According to the illustration in *Theatrum Sabaudiae* this pool already existed in the seventeenth century. Instead of a single jet of water at its centre it had an ornate baroque fountain. Pots of lemon decorated the area around the pool. The spaces on each side now planted with trees were laid out as elaborate *parterres de broderie*. The whole of the eastern boundary, now obscured by trees, is shown as an arcaded retaining wall decorated with gushing fountains. This may be a fanciful elaboration, but if it ever existed it must have been a glorious sight.

The garden set between the retaining walls of the hanging garden and the upper terrace is best seen from above. In the seventeenth-century print the area is depicted as a *broderie* garden. The general layout remains the same with beds set out around a simple central pool. A deep nymphaeum is set into the retaining wall of the hanging garden. Telamones, or male caryatids, stand on either side of the arch and the keystone is decorated with a grotesque mask. Inside, despite the ferocious guardians, there is nothing but an eighteenth-century urn. The *Theatrum Sabaudiae* shows Telamones flanking the shallower

niches at each end of the wall, but if these ever existed they are no longer there.

Below the parterre garden is an area of walled bosco reached by steps concealed behind the box hedge. It was once set out as a series of winding walks lined with box hedges which led to a central knoll. The knoll is still there, and so are the paths, but the whole area is overgrown and neglected.

Returning to the upper terrace one proceeds along the west wall of the palace to the hanging garden. The whole of this side of the palace is given up to a long *limonaia* and a series of frescoed garden rooms cooled by alabaster fountains. All are closed to the public while awaiting restoration. This is a sad loss to the visitor. Their beauty is enhanced by their air of gentle dereliction, and the ivy that swamps the inner wall of the *limonaia*.

The hanging garden that opens out at the end of the terrace represents an impressive feat of seventeenth-century engineering. Unfortunately it is also closed to the public at present, and is in a rather dishevelled state. The geometric layout depicted in the *Theatrum Sabaudiae* has been softened by the trees now dotted about the garden. The view, which must once have been pleasantly open, has been spoilt by modern buildings.

The park can be reached by following the terrace along the east wall of the palace. By turning right under the bridge below one can walk directly to the fountain.

The *Theatrum Sabaudiae* shows an amphitheatre on the site now occupied by the fountain. The semicircular retaining wall behind the pool suggests that this may well have existed and been used as a basis for the new construction. The sculptures, executed by Ignazio and Fil-

ippo Collino in 1770, are said to represent the three tributaries of the Po river.

The fountain and the lawn in front of it form a huge semicircle. They are enclosed by the retaining wall of the curving ramps that lead to the balustraded terrace above. This wall was once decorated with stuccoed panels. Traces of soft yellow plaster mingle with the grey stone that has now been exposed beneath, forming a remarkably beautiful frame for the fountain. Each ramp is planted with an avenue, forming a boundary between the fountain and the wooded parkland to either side.

The park that forms a perfect rectangle stretches out above and beyond the fountain. It was laid out in its present form during the second half of the eighteenth century. Paths wind through the woods in the 'English manner' that was starting to be fashionable at the time. There is a small lake at the far end of the park with two islands on which stand rustic summerhouses.

NEAREST MAJOR TOWN Milan

MAIN FEATURES seventeenth-century island garden, water theatre

PRE-BOOKING no

OWNER Prince Borromeo-Arese

ADDRESS I-28050 Isola Bella; tel.: +39 (0)323 30556

LOCATION the islands lie on the western side of Lago Maggiore. Ferries run from Stresa, Baveno and Pallanza.

Tickets are L13,000 return, valid for unlimited trips between all three islands throughout the day. Boats depart every 30 minutes

OPEN yes

ADMISSION L12,000, children L6000

WHEELCHAIRS no

REFRESHMENTS yes

LAVATORIES yes

Isola Bella is one of the three Borromean islands off Stresa on the western shore of Lago Maggiore. The Borromeo was a Milanese family possessing immense wealth derived from banking operations. Their most famous member is probably San Carlo Borromeo, whose determined attempts to reform the Church led directly to the Counter Reformation. It was his nephew Count Carlo III who in 1632 erected the first building on the island, a simple *casino*. Grander plans soon followed, and the island was slowly transformed by Carlo and his son Count Vitaliano VI.

The Borromeo employed Angelo Crivelli to draw up the original plans. After his death the work was continued by Carlo Fontana and Francesco Castelli, among others. The 40 or so years the garden took to make are easily explained when one considers the task involved – transforming a barren, jagged rock into a base suitable for level terraces up to 30 metres high. Gilbert Burnet, the diarist and bishop, who visited the island in 1685 commented: 'because the figure of the island was not made regular by Nature, they have built great Vaults and Por-

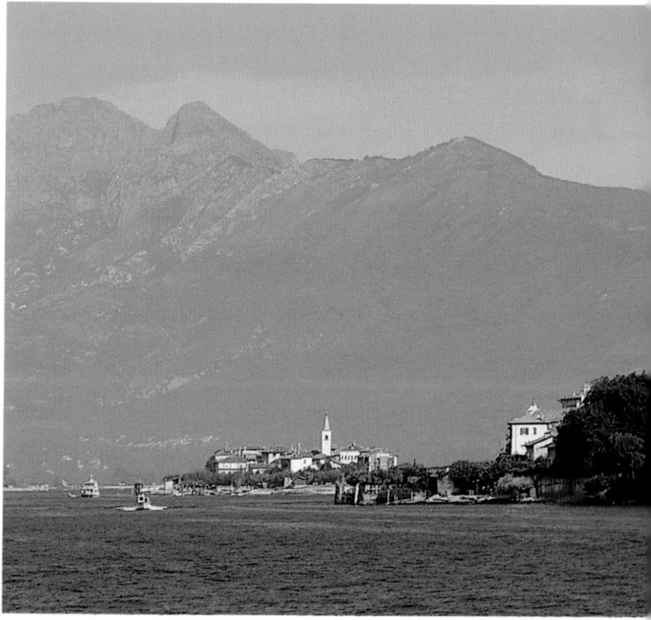

tica's along the rock, which are all made grotes-que, and so they have made it into a regular form by laying earth over these vaults'.

Even before completion the gardens had become famous throughout Europe and were an obligatory halt on the Grand Tour. Countless famous figures have stayed here, including Napoleon and Josephine, after the Battle of Marengo had given them the possession of Italy.

Curiously, Vitaliano halted construction of the palazzo in 1671, and it was not resumed until the 1950s when it was completed by Prince Borromeo-Arese according to the original plans – surely one of the longest building projects in history.

Carlo Borromeo was devoted to his wife Isabella, and originally named the island after her. On his death in 1652 she retired to a convent in nearby Arona. It was not long before the name was shortened to its present and appropriate form. Burnet similarly summarised the effect that the island had on visitors: 'the fragrant smell, the beautiful Prospect, and the delighting Variety that is here makes such a habitation for Summer that perhaps the whole world has nothing like it'.

There is a unique sense of excitement in everything to do with this garden, from the moment of leaving the faded art-nouveau boat station at Baveno. Isola Bella floats among the reflected mountains like the galley it was designed to resemble. Only the ram, at the northern (palazzo) end is lacking. The garden is now entered from the palazzo, which has a useful model of the whole island in a reception room. The entrance is through a most enchanting series of grottoes beneath the palazzo ornamented with shells and pebbles, and containing rare specimens of coral. The submarine colours used for decoration make this a wonderfully refreshing place on the hottest of days.

Nature's failure to make a regular 'figure' of the island meant that

the garden was built markedly off-centre to the palazzo, though on entering the garden through the small courtyard of Diana it is unlikely that one is aware of the change of direction. To the left of the courtyard is the Theatre of Hercules. A central niche in the semicircular wall contains Hercules with club and lion skin, while smaller niches on either side contain lesser divinities.

Having returned to the courtyard of Diana, one climbs the steps to a broad terrace around which stroll the white peacocks claimed to be peculiar to these islands. At the far end rises Isola Bella's most astonishing *coup de théâtre*. This is the water theatre, an enchantingly delicate piece of baroque fantasy. Between the twin flights of stairs to the topmost terrace lies a semicircular wall with niches containing gods, goddesses and enormous scallops from which fountains play. Among them are Mars and Vulcan, and representations of Agriculture and the Arts. From it ascend columns surmounted by putti, each in a different pose, and the whole is topped by the rampant figure of the Borromeo unicorn. The two reclining figures on either side are Toce and Ticino, the two principal rivers that feed Lago Maggiore.

Concealed above and behind the theatre is a broad stone terrace that covers the huge garden reservoir. This terrace is the 'poop' of the galley, complete even to the figurehead. This bears the Borromeo crown and their motto 'humilitas' – rather less than apt in these gorgeous surroundings. From here one may look down over the 'stern' and count the ten terraces descending to the water's edge. Two hexagonal towers stand below on either side, one a summerhouse, the other containing the pumps for the reservoir.

On descending the steps on the eastern side one arrives at the lower parterre garden on the fifth terrace. There is an aviary on one side; the

other side overlooks the orange garden. The espaliered fruit trees have to be protected by temporary roofs during the winter.

Continuing round, one reaches the southern tip of the island, laid out with *parterres de broderie*. The western side is the most recently planted, during the last century; the exotic trees and shrubs include camellia and magnolia. The planting elsewhere in the garden is much as it always was, though the trees have grown so large that they have blurred the starkly dramatic lines of the original plan. Burnet refers to the walls as 'close covered with Oranges and Citrons'. Charles de Brosses, in 1739, describes the terraces as having trellises of jasmine, pomegranates or oranges and the balustrades as being edged with pots of flowers. The mild climate means that garden designers here have always used colour with a freedom not found in the rest of Italy.

Exit is from the west side on the fifth terrace, through the village that until recently was occupied solely by the retainers of the Borromeo.

palazzo reale

NEAREST MAJOR TOWN Turin
MAIN FEATURES seventeenth-century
French garden by André Le Nôtre
PRE-BOOKING no
OWNER the State
ADDRESS Piazzetta Realei, I-10122
Torino; tel.: +39 (0)11 4361455
LOCATION the palazzo is easily found
in the centre of Turin with
a street map bought from any
giornalaio (news kiosk). It is

nearly always possible to park in the
piazza in front of the palazzo
OPEN garden, spring and summer
9.00–19.00; palazzo, Wednesday to
Monday 09.00–12.20, 14.20–17.40
ADMISSION garden, free;
palazzo L8000, children free
WHEELCHAIRS yes
REFRESHMENTS no
LAVATORIES yes

The garden of Palazzo Reale was designed by André Le Nôtre for Vittorio Amadeo II, Duke of Savoy, and was laid out between 1697 and 1702. The site for the new garden was generally acknowledged as 'difficult', consisting of the irregular space between the royal palace and the city walls. The size of the site had been effectively tripled when Carlo Emanuele I, Vittorio Amadeo's father, demolished the fortifications to the east of the palace and replaced them with new walls in a slightly different position. It was evidently his intention to replace the existing baroque garden, thought to have been designed by Carlo Morello, with a larger and more grandiose design. The preliminary work of levelling the site and filling in the holes left by the demolition of the original walls began in 1675. However, Carlo Emanuele's death put an end to further progress. Vittorio Amadeo was subsequently involved in a disastrous war with the French and no further thought was given to the new garden until after the Treaty of Ryswick in 1697.

Vittorio Amadeo approached Le Nôtre through the Piedmontese

ambassador in Paris. Almost exactly 20 years earlier Le Nôtre had been to Rome. On his return to France he pronounced the Italians 'absolutely ignorant' of the art of making gardens. It was perhaps with a sense of satisfaction at the thought of making a 'real' garden in Italy that he presented his proposed plans to the ambassador. The plans were duly sent on to the duke, accompanied by a letter in which the ambassador told him of the curiosity that the project was arousing in the French court.

Le Nôtre, who was 85 years old in 1697, did not travel to Turin. Having gained the duke's approval of his plans, he entrusted their implementation to his pupil, De Marne. In a letter to one of the duke's ministers he described De Marne as 'un très abile et honneste homme fort sage ...', and with touching concern begged that he should be given every comfort during his stay in Turin.

De Marne arrived in the city in October 1697. In December he returned to Paris to consult Le Nôtre and continued to travel between Paris and Turin for the next six months. There can be no doubt that De Marne was capable of implementing Le Nôtre's plans, but as a mark of respect for his teacher he chose to refer any difficulties that arose on site directly to him.

The essential layout of the garden was complete within the year. No further record of De Marne's presence in Turin can be found after June 1698, when he ordered 130 octagonal stone bases for pots, 160 square ones, and a quantity of marble for fountains and benches.

After De Marne's departure Enrico Duparc was director of the garden. He was an architect and is thought to have supervised the completion of Le Nôtre's plans, adding some finishing touches of his own.

Over the years the garden has undergone alteration. The urns and statues that stand among the trees are an eighteenth-century addition. The eastern end of the long entrance avenue was destroyed during the nineteenth century and in 1920 Le Nôtre's design was cut in half by a new road linking Piazza Castello to Corso San Maurizio and Corso Regina Margherita.

The basis of Le Nôtre's design was to create three different areas in the garden, each with its own vista. The first was to the north of the palazzo, immediately in front of the gateway that leads from the inner courtyard. Although the planting may have changed, the long beds of the rose garden are much as they were conceived. The area is no longer decorated with rows of pots between the beds, but lime and plane trees still bound the garden to the right, just as Le Nôtre intended.

The second area is laid out at right angles to the rose garden. The original design was for two extensive parterres laid out to the east of the palace, and linked to it by a short flight of balustraded steps. The parterres have been replaced by two lawns divided by a gravel walk. The circular pool on the far side of the parterre garden is ornamented with a massive rococo fountain attributed to Simone Martinez, who was director of the House of Savoy's sculpture studio. The principal figures are vast tritons playing conch shells. Dolphins, flowers and nymphs create a tangle of activity at water level, quite out of keeping with the simplicity of the rest of the garden.

The last of Le Nôtre's three vistas was formed by six radiating avenues, one more than 400 metres long. When the garden was divided by the new road at the beginning of last century, part of it was simply absorbed into the city. However, what remains of the great avenues constitutes perhaps the most beautiful, and the most recognisably French, aspect of the garden. The climate of northern

Italy favours deciduous trees, and they are widely used these gardens. However, it was not usual to plant them in avenues. The evergreen cypress was preferred for such 'architectural' features.

We visited the garden in hazy autumn sunlight and were delighted by its simple lines and the charming eighteenth-century statues standing in the dappled shade. It is a municipal garden, however, and it can suffer from the lack of atmosphere that so easily afflicts gardens that have been for many years without an owner..

NEAREST MAJOR TOWN Milan

MAIN FEATURES nineteenth-century garden terraced in the Renaissance manner, spectacular views over Lago Maggiore

PRE-BOOKING yes

OWNER Regione di Piemonte

ADDRESS Via S Remigio 9, I-28048 Pallanza-Verbania; tel.: +39 (0)323 504401

LOCATION Pallanza is on the west side of Lago Maggiore on the SS34. Turn left immediately after Piazza Giovanni XXIII, taking Via Cavallina. Take the narrow lanes up the hill following signs for the 'provincia VCO'. Do not go up the Salita San Remigio

OPEN appointment only; contact Comune di Verbania, Ufficio Turismo, C.so Zanitello, 6/8–28922 Verbania; tel.: +39 (0)323 503249, fax.: (0)323 556669

ADMISSION FEE on application

WHEELCHAIRS no

REFRESHMENTS no

LAVATORIES no

Villa San Remigio is named after the little church that stands by the garden. Its history is entwined with the lives of two families who bought land on the Castagnola hill above Lago Maggiore. Peter Browne, a British diplomat of Irish origin, bought his plot of land in 1859. Shortly afterwards he built a Swiss chalet there, to which he retired with his large family. The fields adjoining the Browne's property were bought by a Neapolitan marquis, Federico della Valle di Casanova. It was not long before one of Browne's daughters fell in love with the marquis and the marriage resulted in a son, Silvio. Browne's eldest son, Dionysius, was already married. Sophie Browne, his second child, was destined to carry the union between the Brownes and Casanova into a second generation by marrying Silvio to become the della Valle di Casanovas. The land belonging to the two families was finally merged, and Sophie and Silvio began what was to be their life's

piedmont

work. In 1903 the Swiss chalet was demolished for Sophie's and Silvio's new villa, which was to by built in the Renaissance manner by a local firm. In 1905 they constructed the terrace behind the villa that overlooks the lake.

Little is known of the massive task of terracing the hillside to the north and south of the house. It is said that Sophie built a wood and cloth model of the terraces in front of the house and adjusted the model until she was happy with its effect at all times of day. Even the effect of moonlight on the terraces was studied before the garden was built. By 1916 both villa and garden were complete. The garden, tended by 30 gardeners, was open to the public during the week.

Sophie died aged 100 in 1960. In 1977, San Remigio was bought by the State, and it is now used as their regional offices.

'We are Silvio and Sophie della Valle di Casanova. Childhood united us, and this garden was born of the dreams that we shared in our youth. We planned it as children, and as man and wife we have created it.' This is a translation of the introduction to the garden engraved on a plaque behind the villa. The fruit of Silvio and Sophie's youthful dreams is a romantic mixture of styles that ranges from the sacred grove to the winding paths of the eighteenth-century English park. Lago Maggiore provides a breathtakingly beautiful backdrop.

Although the planting of the garden is well maintained by the five gardeners now employed here, its structure has reached such a critical point of decay that some areas have had to be closed to the public. It is ironic that the crumbling steps and overgrown paths should seem to heighten the della Valle's romantic intention.

Sophie's carefully planned 'Renaissance' terraces lie below the southern façade of the villa. There are six in all linked to the house by

a double flight of balustraded steps. The first terrace is characterised by mock-Roman fountains set in niches in the sustaining wall. The niches are decorated with mosaic festoons and dolphins. A series of shell seats supported by dolphin pedestals set along the edge of a green lawn carpet creates the impression of an outdoor drawing room accentuated by a curious armchair made of clipped yew. Statues of the four seasons by Francesco Rizzi – the eighteenth-century Paduan sculptor – crown the other garden wall.

The next terrace acts as a ceiling for the glorious winter garden that lies beneath. A vaulted grotto has been dug out beneath the terrace and sealed with a glass wall. A stream runs through it, creating a marvellously warm and steamy atmosphere ideal for growing subtropical plants. The marquis took several romantic pictures of his wife amid ferns and orchids, which can still be seen in the archives of the museum in Pallanza.

The Hour Garden, so named because of the circular stone sundial at its centre, occupies the same terrace as the winter garden. The sundial is decorated with the signs of the zodiac and an inscription that, roughly translated, reads: 'Put here by Silvio and Sophie so that the new light of day may dispel the shadows of fled hours'. The statues that decorate the balustrade are by Orazio Marinali and represent Juno, Bacchus, Venus and Pluto.

A second winter garden, twice the length of the first, stands above the lowest terrace. Known as the Garden of Happiness, it has a series of *parterres de broderie* laid out around a central pool, and is divided by pebble mosaic paths. A magnificent fountain, 'The Triumph of Diana' by Riccardo Ripamonti, stands in the pool. The goddess stands in a shell chariot pulled by two web-footed horses.

Wrought-iron balconies overlook the lowest terrace, or Garden of Sadness, and the steps down to it are guarded by griffins with iron wings. While the Garden of Happiness was originally planted with innumerable roses, the Garden of Sadness has always been filled with mournful evergreens. It is occupied by two pools set in lawns bounded by box and an elaborate wrought-iron fence. A nymphaeum, decorated with mosaics and the family crest, shelters a statue of Hercules killing the Hydra by Giovanni Marchiori. Stone seats shaded by topiary columns are set against the retaining wall.

Next to the little church of San Remigio, reached by a path down through the woods from the second terrace, is an area seemingly intended as a sacred grove. Cypresses shade a simple central pool, and a statue of Pan by Ripamonti stands guard. The true scale of these gardens is only apparent when one realises that the entire hillside below the villa was cultivated as an 'English' garden that ran down to the lake. The winding paths, steps and terraces that led down through the trees are now largely overgrown. The woods are made up of a strange mixture of bog oak, cedar, chestnut, bamboo, Japanese privet, camphor and rhododendron.

Above the English garden is a long, arcaded gallery where ivy and wisteria run riot. Steps lead up through a tunnel to the terrace behind the villa.

The two 'seventeenth-century' terraces to the north of the villa are known as the 'Garden of Sighs' and the 'Garden of Memories'. Among the statues in the former are the effigies of Sophie and Silvio.

NEAREST MAJOR TOWN Milan

MAIN FEATURES large twentieth-century botanic gardens, outstanding collections of flowering trees and shrubs

PRE-BOOKING no

OWNER the State

ADDRESS Via V Veneto 111, I-28048 Pallanza-Verbania; tel.: +39 (0)323 404555/556667

LOCATION Pallanza is on the west side of Lago Maggiore on the SS34. The gardens are well signposted on the main road. They may also be reached by ferry from Stresa, Baveno or Pallanza

OPEN April to October, 8.30–18.00

ADMISSION L10,000

WHEELCHAIRS yes

REFRESHMENTS yes

LAVATORIES yes

The gardens owe their existence to the remarkable energy of one man, Captain Neil McEacharn. The only son of a wealthy Scottish businessman, he found the Scottish social climate unwelcoming for a man of his tastes and habits. In 1930, when already a knowledgeable plantsman, he bought an estate on the western side of Lago Maggiore, bordering the Villa San Remigio (page 39). This was the first of several acquisitions of land that by 1935 had increased the size of the estate to c. 40 hectares. Several years of energetic landscaping followed. The ground was largely cleared, terraces prepared, reservoirs built and the winding valley (the 'Valletta') was dug. The work was carried out under the directorship of Henry Cocker, who had trained at Kew and had gained experience of Italian conditions at La Mortola (page 68). He remained as director for 26 years, taking responsibility for much of the planting and layout.

McEacharn, as a passionate botanist, had no taste for the formal Italianate style adopted by his neighbour and friend Sophie della Valle di Casanova. In any event the nature of the landscape suggested the naturalistic approach typical of many Scottish gardens. As indeed did the climate; 2.3 metres of annual rainfall and 20 degrees of frost during the long winters. He imported a great number of rhododendrons and azaleas from his home in Scotland, and brought in other plants from all over the world; there are some 20,000 species represented, many propagated here from seed.

The gardens survived the Second World War largely undamaged thanks to the efforts of McEacharn's secretary and administrator, Antonio Cappelletto. In 1951, McEacharn donated Villa Taranto to the Italian State.

The garden of Villa Taranto covers c. 40 hectares on which there are no less than 8 kilometres of roads and paths. These impressive statistics must convince even the hardiest of garden visitors that this is not a site to be conquered in one visit.

Taranto is a plantsman's paradise. The climate, with its hot summers and high rainfall, promotes extraordinarily rapid growth of plants and trees from all over the world. The size and variety of the trees are immediately striking as one enters the drive, which is lined with an avenue of conifers. Blue, silver, green and golden varieties of spruce are interplanted with cypress, stone and umbrella pine. Combined with the technicolour bedding plants that were Cocker's trademark, the effect is striking.

The rhododendron wood beyond the conifers has species in flower from February to June. Above it is a large grove of magnolia that contains almost every known species: it is world famous. Most of the plants grow to three or four times their normal size, many reaching colossal heights.

At the head of the man-made valley is a bridge linking the villa to the formal gardens. A long flight of steps up the farthest side of the valley leads to a large lawn. The surrounding beds are filled with a lavish planting of tulip in the spring. The nineteenth-century villa is visible beyond the lawn.

The formal gardens can be reached from the lawn by crossing the

piedmont

bridge over the valley. A channel of water runs through them, culminating in a life-size bronze of a fisher boy by Vincenzo Gemito. A succession of bedding plants fill the beds to each side throughout the year. A horseshoe-shaped stone pergola is covered in different species of wisteria and yellow and scarlet bignonia. The pool, with its massive lotus flowers, is another striking feature in this area of the garden. The water is drained from the pool each winter so that the lotus tubers can be covered with a protective blanket of dead leaves.

To appreciate all that this garden has to offer, it is essential to buy the guide book on sale there. Cocker was proud that some species of plant were in flower at Villa Taranto throughout the year. As a result, the garden is worth a visit at any time during its open season.

lombardy (lombardia)

Lombardy (Lombardia) lies in the north of the country. Its landscape comprises the Alps, the Italian lakes and the vast flat valley of the River Po. The climate, like that of its neighbour Piedmont, can be harsh in winter, with a high annual rainfall.

The region's varied geography has given rise to a range of gardens that cannot be classified under any one stylistic group. The impact of the Renaissance was keenly felt in the area, and towards the end of the sixteenth century gardens took on the elaborate architectural appearance that originated in Rome.

Edith Wharton was the first to identify the danger to the gardens of those with too much, rather than too little, money. The ease with which their owners could embrace changing fashions led to regular bouts of destruction and rebuilding. This was certainly the case in Lombardy, where many sixteenth-century gardens were destroyed during the eighteenth century to accommodate fashionable 'English' parks. In the Po valley this operation was rendered all the easier by the flat terrain.

NEAREST MAJOR TOWN Como

MAIN FEATURES lakeside setting, small eighteenth-century formal garden, fine botanical gardens

PRE-BOOKING no

OWNER the State

ADDRESS Via Regina 2, I-22019 Tremezzo; tel.: +39 (0)344 40405/41011

LOCATION Tremezzo is 30 kilometres north of Como on the western side of Lago di Como. From Como take the ss340 for Menaggio and Gravedona. The villa is clearly signposted and is by Lago di Como between Tremezzo and Cadenabbia

OPEN April to September, 9.00–18.00; March and October, 9.00–11.30, 14.00–16.30

ADMISSION L10,000, children L5000 (free under 6 years of age)

WHEELCHAIRS no

REFRESHMENTS no

LAVATORIES yes

Construction of Villa Carlotta was begun in 1690 for Marshal Giorgio Clerici, architect unknown, and was completed by 1745. Fifty years later it passed by marriage into the hands of Giovanni Sommariva, who among other alterations added the unfortunate pediment and clock to the villa. In 1843 the property was given as a wedding present by Princess Marianna of Prussia to her daughter Charlotte, Duchess of Saxe-Meiningen, hence its name. She and her husband were responsible for the creation of the large landscape garden with its wide range of species, made feasible by the mild climate. On the outbreak of the First World War the villa was confiscated by the Italian government and has remained State property. Since 1927 the house and grounds have been carefully maintained under the management of the Ente Villa Carlotta.

Before buying an entrance ticket it is worth crossing the road (taking your life in your hands) and standing on the steps of the watergate.

lombardy (lombardia)

This would have been the original arrival point, having enjoyed the view of the villa with its mountain background reflected in the lake. From here the perfect symmetry of the double stairs leading to the villa is best appreciated. The fine wrought-iron gates, with their gilded initial 'c's and columns surmounted by personifications of the Seasons, are no longer opened. The present entrance lies to the left by the neo-classical Sommariva family chapel.

Inside the original entrance lies a small central pool with a delightful fountain of a boy with a dolphin. This is surrounded by box hedges laid out in the form of coronets, filled with begonia. On either side dense *boschi* hem in the visitor. These replace what was once a delicate *parterre de broderie* running the width of the garden.

Three narrow terraces lie between this area and the villa. The geometrical lines of the ascending balustrade are softened by the climbing roses, vines and trailing geraniums with which they are covered. Fern-filled wall fountains refresh the visitor climbing to the villa, while a pergola on the second level leads past orange and lemon trees. In this temperate climate these have been planted directly in the ground rather than in pots.

Passing through the villa, with its collection of statues by the eighteenth-century sculptor Antonio Canova, among others, one finds a dark grotto set in the cliff behind the house. Looking back, the villa gives the impression of being filled with light.

Turning to the right at this point takes one into the heart of the landscape garden, which is maintained by a staff of ten. The outstanding collection of azalea and rhododendron is worth visiting when the plants are at their peak from late April to half way through May.

villa cicogna

NEAREST MAJOR TOWN Varese
MAIN FEATURES sixteenth-century garden in a rural setting with fine views, sunken garden, water staircase
PRE-BOOKING no (see below)
OWNER Cicogna-Mozzoni
ADDRESS Piazza Cicogna 8, I-21050 Bisuschio; tel./fax.: +39 (0)332 471134
LOCATION Bisuschio is 8 kilometres north of Varese on the SS344 for Porto Ceresio and Ponte Tresa. The villa is on the left just through Bisuschio. Parking is opposite the villa's entrance
OPEN Sunday and public holidays, 31 March to 27 October, 9.30–12.00, 14.30–19.00; weekdays (groups only) by arrangement; contact +39 (0)332 471134
ADMISSION L7000
WHEELCHAIRS no
REFRESHMENTS no
LAVATORIES yes

Villa Cicogna has been the home of the Cicogna family for more than 400 years. It was originally built as a hunting lodge by the Mozzoni in the fifteenth century. Over the years they used the lodge with increasing frequency, eventually expanding it, having it frescoed inside and out, and turning it into their main residence. In 1592 Asciano Mozzoni died, leaving the villa to his daughter Angela. It was through her marriage to Gianpietro Cicogna that the property came to Cicogna hands. They transformed it into a magnificent Renaissance villa and laid out most of the existing garden. Sadly, there is no record of the name of the garden architect employed. The terrace garden north of the villa was a seventeenth-century addition, and in the eighteenth century the woods above the villa were transformed into an 'English' park.

The gardens are laid out on the side of a steep slope. The visitor enters through an arcaded courtyard, the arcades exquisitely frescoed with a trellis of leaves and flowers, putti and peacocks heralding one's first glimpse of the garden, bathed in sunlight beyond the shadowy

courtyard. This garden is enclosed on one side by the courtyard and the villa, and on the other three sides by high walls. On the right the retaining wall of the upper terrace is decorated with niches containing busts and statues. The boundary wall on the opposite side of the garden is covered in ivy. It has a nymphaeum set into it that shelters a statue of Mercury. The far wall, which is of equal height, contains a grotto. On our visit it was being restored and it contained nothing but a complex web of pipes for *giochi d'acqua*. The garden is laid out in a regular pattern of box hedges, lawns and colourful beds of begonia and geranium. Below the retaining wall are two rectangular balustraded fishponds of considerable size. The fountains at the centre of each pool fill the enclosed space with the sound of running water. It is fitting that this garden, with its peace and privacy, should be linked to the lower and less formal part of the villa. The reception rooms of the *piano nobile* open on to the wide upper terrace, which is very different in scale and purpose to the intimate garden below.

The terrace is linked to the sunken garden by a flight of steps that leads up through a tunnel to the left of the grotto. One enters the tunnel through a pair of wrought-iron gates decorated with the stork (*cicogna*), the family coat of arms.

The balustraded terrace runs the width of the garden. At its southern end it gives a vantage point from which to enjoy the bright parterre beds and shimmering pools below. It passes between the villa and the base of the water staircase, ending beyond the boundary of the seventeenth-century terrace garden to the north of the villa. The terrace represents that essential element of a Renaissance garden: a sheltered walk offering views over the garden and surrounding countryside. On a clear day Lago di Lugano, on the border of Italy and Switzerland, can be seen in the distance. A raised rose walk runs parallel to the terrace, broken only at its mid-point by two supine maidens who flank the base of the water staircase.

The staircase was designed to be seen from the windows of the *piano nobile*, and it is only from inside the villa that the intended perspective can be truly appreciated. Rising steeply from its base to a pavilion on the crest of the hill, it creates an effective visual link between the lower garden and the bosco above. This exploitation of the natural landscape to architectural ends betrays the influence that the great gardens of the Roman Renaissance were already having on the designers of the north.

The water feeding the staircase originally came from a spring and was carried through the woods in a little aqueduct. It is now pumped up from below, but it is fun to trace the old route through the woods of the 'English' park.

At its northern end the terrace leads into a sloping grove of yew and beech. A path leads through the grove, past the remains of a balustraded terrace and fountain, and up to the pavilion at the head of the water staircase. Beyond the pavilion the bosco merges with the eighteenth-century park. Today red squirrels abound in these woods, where once the Mozzoni and their guests hunted bear and wild boar.

NEAREST MAJOR TOWN Como
MAIN FEATURES lakeside setting, fine sixteenth-century double water staircase, hotel
PRE-BOOKING yes, unless using hotel facilities
OWNER Villa d'Este
ADDRESS I-22012 Cernobbio, Lago di Como
LOCATION Cernobbio is 5 kilometres north of Como on the western side of

Lago di Como. From Como take the SS340 for Menaggio and Gravedona. The villa is clearly signposted in Cernobbio
OPEN March to November; open to hotel guests or by appointment; tel.: +39 (0)31 511471/512471
ADMISSION free
WHEELCHAIRS yes
REFRESHMENTS yes
LAVATORIES yes

Despite its name, Villa d'Este has never been connected with the Este of Ferrara. It was built in 1568 for Tolomeo Gallio, of a Como family, on his appointment as cardinal. He commissioned the Lombard architect Pellegrino Tibaldi to build him three villas on Lago di Como, the others being at Lenno and Gravedona. Villa Garrovo, as the villa at Cernobbio was originally known, became his principal residence. After the cardinal's death, it fell gradually into neglect, eventually passing into the hands of the Jesuits.

At the end of the eighteenth century it was acquired by Marquis Bartolomeo Calderara for his wife Vittoria Peluso, a famous dancer known as 'La Pelusina'. She restored the villa and commenced the alteration of the gardens, and was also responsible for the extraordinary mock fortifications built to flatter her second husband Dominique Pirro who had been one of Napoleon's generals.

In 1815 Villa Garrovo was bought by Princess Caroline of Brunswick, the dissolute, eccentric and understandably neglected wife of the

Prince Regent. In a fanciful moment she changed its name to Villa d'Este, and restyled both villa and garden in the fashion of the time. After her death the villa changed hands several times. In 1856 it was first launched as a hotel by Baron Ciani. Following a short ownership by the Empress Maria Fedorowna of Russia, it was relaunched in 1873, and is now among Europe's most famous hotels.

In the course of its many changes of function and ownership nearly all of Tibaldi's garden has been lost. However, the superb double water staircase is among the few surviving original features. Unusually for a garden of such pronounced Roman influence, this is off-centre to the villa, Tibaldi undoubtedly intending that the outstanding view of the lake should not be obstructed. As a result, the visitor approaching by water could have gazed straight up the long avenue of cypress and magnolia to the nymphaeum at the summit. It is well worth enjoying this wonderful perspective by having tea by the lake as we did.

The lawn was originally, and until quite recently, occupied by four large parterres. Beyond the lawn, and framing the water staircase, is a series of splendidly theatrical 'wings', decorated in shell and pebble mosaic and topped with obelisks. They were once intended to be roofed in to form garden pavilions linking the villa to the present *limonaia*, but were never completed.

Steps lead up around a central fishpond to the foot of the water staircase. This crosses the lakeside road by a bridge. It is unusual in being a double stair, so that the visitor has the charming experience of climbing the broad *tapis vert*, striped with sunlight and shadow, with the sight and sound of falling water on either side. At the top stands an elaborately decorated and bat-filled nymphaeum containing a dramatic statue of the dying Hercules, maddened with pain, hurling his companion Lichas into the water.

On either side of the avenue the grounds have been terraced and originally were planted with olive or vine. A bridge leads across the Garrovo stream to the maze of paths with which the cliffs are covered. These lead to the forts, battlements, pavilions and waterfalls that exemplify the fevered excesses of the Romantic imagination.

villa della porta-bozzolo

NEAREST MAJOR TOWN Varese

MAIN FEATURES striking seventeenth-century terraced garden in a rural setting, oak avenue, frescoed apse

PRE-BOOKING yes

OWNER Fondo per l'Ambiente Italiano (FAI)

ADDRESS Viale Bozzolo, I-21030 Casalzuigno; tel.: +39 (0)332 624136

LOCATION Casalzuigno is c. 20 kilometres north-west of Varese. From Varese take the SS394 for Laveno and after 17 kilometres turn right for Brenta and Casalzuigno. The villa is signposted to the left on the far side of the village. If coming from Milan follow the A8 for Sesto Calende. Take the Sesto C-Vergiate exit in the direction of Besozzo-Laveno. Follow signs to Gemonio and then Luino-Valcuvia and Casalzuigno

OPEN Tuesday to Sunday, February to September, 10.00–18.00, October to mid-December, 10.00–17.00 (villa closed 13.00–14.00)

ADMISSION L7000, children aged 6–10 years L2000

WHEELCHAIRS no

REFRESHMENTS no

LAVATORIES yes

Very little is known of the history of Il Bozzolo and its garden. The villa was built at the beginning of the sixteenth century for the della Porta family, and the garden was laid out during the first half of the seventeenth century. Its design is sometimes attributed to Gianangelo della Porta.

The property passed by marriage to the Ferrari family at the end of the eighteenth century. For most of this century it was owned by the Bozzolo family and in 1989 was acquired by the Fondo per l'Ambiente Italiano (FAI), the Italian equivalent of The British National Trust.

Il Bozzolo is set on the side of a steep, wooded valley overlooking the Alps. It is an overwhelming landscape, and yet through its simple and perfectly balanced design the garden succeeds in framing and incorpo-

lombardy (lombardia)

rating its surroundings without being dwarfed by them. In so doing it exemplifies that peculiarly Italian skill of creating an absolute bond between the layout of a garden and the landscape surrounding it.

A powerful horizontal perspective is formed by four stone terraces running the width of the garden. They, with their balustrades and the graceful flight of steps linking them, can be seen spreading out across the hillside from the road below. What cannot be appreciated from below is their surprising length and depth. Each terrace extends away from the steps beyond the line of vision and has a breadth of c. 9 metres. They are rather like a series of enclosed gardens, filled with the sound of running water by the shell fountains that decorate the walls. On each retaining wall espaliered fruit trees flourish, while the balustrades are decorated with stone urns overflowing with fruit. At the end of each balustrade a putto stands as a guardian over the steps, each striking a different pose.

The horizontal perspective created by the terrace seems to establish the garden's place in the landscape, while the avenue of cypresses cutting through the woods on the hillside above succeeds in drawing that landscape into the garden. The avenue is now largely overgrown, which is scarcely surprising when one considers that the whole property has for years been maintained by a single gardener. However, while the path of the avenue may still be traced its effect is felt in the garden.

The villa is not incorporated into this powerfully linear design. It stands below the terraces, facing away from the central perspective and overlooking a small lawn that once may have been planted as parterres. Across the lawn a magnificent avenue of oaks leads away to a frescoed apse. The avenue is more than 90 metres long, and the oak trees create a mottled shade quite unlike the zebra stripes of a cypress avenue. The apse, which is frescoed with gods and goddesses in a sylvan setting, provides a delightful setting for the occasional summer concert.

Between the terraces and the wooded hillside is a sloping, semicircular meadow. It represents the most curious and perhaps the most skilled aspect of the garden's design. It is divided from the surrounding countryside by a low stone wall and bank. The addition of cypresses, planted to follow the line of the wall, strengthens the visual boundary between the garden and hillside. By enclosing a portion of the surrounding countryside, the architect hit on the simplest possible way of increasing the apparent size of the garden, thus bringing it into proportion with the landscape beyond.

The meadow is crowned by a double flight of balustraded steps leading to a small terrace. Signora Bozzolo told us that her children used to swim in the pool immediately below the terrace: a perfect vantage point from which to look back at the garden and to enjoy the grandeur of its setting.

liguria

regional introduction

Liguria lies between Piedmont and the sea. Sheltered by mountains from the cold northerly winds, and facing south over the Mediterranean, its climate is mild throughout the year.

Genoa, the capital, has varied in importance over the centuries. In the fourteenth century it was defeated by Venice in the struggle for maritime power. The city enjoyed a burst of confidence and a brief period of independence during the sixteenth century under the leadership of Admiral Andrea Doria.

The ideal climate along this coast has always inspired the creation of gardens in a wide range of styles. Genoa, once famous as a city of gardens stretching from the sea to the hills above, lost almost all of its gardens to nineteenth-century urban development and few remain. Doria's palazzo, often described by travellers as being among the finest Renaissance gardens in Italy, survived to the present century but the upper garden was destroyed within months of Edith Wharton's visit in 1903. The lower garden survived until quite recently when, with an insensitivity to their heritage that defies belief, the Genoese built a motorway flyover across it, and turned what remained into an open-air cinema.

NEAREST MAJOR TOWN Genoa
MAIN FEATURES typical Genoese
hanging garden
PRE-BOOKING no
OWNER Municipio di Genova
ADDRESS Via Garibaldi, 1-916124
Genova; tel.: +39 (0)10 20981
LOCATION Via Garibaldi is in the old
town in the centre of Genoa. The

easiest entry is through the Galleria di
Palazzo Bianco at no. 11
OPEN Monday to Friday, 8.00–17.30;
Saturday, 8.00–12.00
ADMISSION free (garden only)
WHEELCHAIRS no
REFRESHMENTS no
LAVATORIES yes

During the sixteenth century Genoa was undergoing a renaissance of its own. In 1528 the Genoese Republic had been set on a firmer footing under the rule of Admiral Andrea Doria, and the political stability that ensued resulted in a rapid expansion of the city. Genoa at this time lacked native artists and architects of distinction. This was a not uncommon situation in such a great mercantile city, whose attentions and energies were naturally directed outwards. Exceptionally lucky in their choice, they commissioned, among others, Galeazzo Alessi who in 1550 laid out the Strada Nuova (now Via Garibaldi). From 1558 he designed a number of the palazzi that line it, coping brilliantly with the difficulties of the steeply sloping site. This is the earliest example in Europe of such a unified scheme of construction under a single architect.

Palazzo Doria Tursi was built in 1564 for Prince Niccolò Grimaldo. Thirty years later it passed into the hands of the Doria family, who added the loggias on either side. Since the revolution of 1848 it has belonged to the city of Genoa.

The steep hillside above the Via Garibaldi is densely covered with the buildings of Renaissance Genoa. Little space was available for gar-

liguria

dens. Alessi and his fellow architects solved the problem by making use of the hanging garden. The result is an extraordinary interlocking pattern of buildings and gardens. In this intensely urban environment almost every window overlooks a green space, a need too often ignored by contemporary planners. Few of these gardens, however, have survived unchanged. The earliest to remain in its original condition, that of Palazzo Podestà, is sadly no longer accessible to visitors.

Palazzo Doria Tursi's twin gardens lie on either side of the palace at the level of the *piano nobile* and consequently overlook the street. Only the left-hand garden is open to the public. On entering from the Palazzo Bianco one meets a small octagonal fishpond with a sea-horse fountain and a pebble-mosaic surround. Typically, statuary in these urban gardens is small, creating an illusion of space. The dwarf palms and clipped laurels surrounding the fountain build on this effect.

At the open (southern) end of the garden overlooking the street are two enormous horsechestnuts that provide shade in summer, so alleviating the heat trapped between the towering limestone walls on either side. Beyond the trees runs a balustrade decorated with urns and globes of box. From here one can look straight into the first-floor windows of the palazzo across the street. The loggia added by the Doria extends into the garden at this end of the palazzo. Concerts are held here in summer.

The remainder of the garden is composed of low box hedges and gravel paths. At the northern end is the high retaining wall of the terrace above (part of the garden of the Palazzo Bianco). At its base stands a fountain in the figure of a woman whose breast spurts a fine jet of water into the pool beneath. This creates a striking effect set against the dark green foliage with which the wall is covered.

villa durazzo pallavicini

NEAREST MAJOR TOWN Genoa
MAIN FEATURES neoclassical garden,
lake, temples
PRE-BOOKING no
OWNER Comune di Genova
ADDRESS Via Pallavicini 11–13,
I-16155 Genova-Pegli;
tel.: +39 (0)10 6982865
LOCATION Pegli is c. 10 kilometres
west of the centre of Genoa towards
Savona. The villa entrance is close to
the station and next to the PCI
(Communist Party) club
OPEN Tuesday to Sunday, April to
September, 9.00–19.00; October to
March, 10.00–17.00. The botanic
gardens are open to groups by
arrangement; tel.: +39 (0)10 209814
ADMISSION L7000, children L5000 (free
under 6 years of age)
WHEELCHAIRS no
REFRESHMENTS no
LAVATORIES no

By the early nineteenth century the Italian Riviera had already become
a magnet for foreign visitors, largely because of the mildness of its
climate and its spectacular exotic gardens. It was with this in mind that
Marquis Ignazio Pallavicini decided to create a romantic park near his
villa at Pegli in 1837. He employed the painter Michele Carizio to draw
up the designs. On completion the garden was opened to the public
and was instantly successful both with the local population and with
the increasing numbers of foreign visitors. It has remained open for
the last 150 years and, despite the graffiti, it retains all its slightly
vulgar charm.

Edith Wharton visited the gardens, commenting: 'a brummagem
creation … to which the guidebooks still send throngs of unsuspecting
tourists, who come back imagining that this tawdry jumble of weeping willows and Chinese pagodas, mock Gothic ruins and exotic vegetation, represents the typical "Italian garden"'. Written at the turn of

liguria

the century, her comments do less than justice to a garden that has given pleasure for so long to so many. It is important to remember that Carizio's secondary occupation was as a theatrical set designer and the garden perhaps should be regarded as an absurd and two-dimensional joke.

A long avenue winds up to the villa between ilexes and palms, crossing the railway *en route*. It opens eventually on to the terrace in front of the villa. The view over the Bay of Genoa must once have been superb, but one now looks out over the shoddy postwar building that has infested every bit of ground between the villa and the sea. Below lies the botanical garden of one Clelia Grimaldi. A statue commemorates her botanical knowledge.

The current way of entering the garden seems unnecessarily complex. Along a fire-escape attached to the cliff face below the villa, past palms and camphor trees, up a steep flight of steps past the neo-gothic chapel and finally into a long avenue leading to the entrance of the garden proper. This is a neo-classical arch with a pavilion above. A Latin inscription advises the visitor as follows: 'Farewell to those urban cares that trouble the soul; I am called by the high mountains, woods, fountains and all that is sublime and eloquent in Nature and raises the spirit to God'. A box walk beyond this leads past a simple fountain under the overhanging trees to a matching arch at the far end. As one passes through it, suddenly it is transformed into a rustic hut. This apparently whimsical juxtaposition perhaps offers a clue to the designer's intention. Here there is no place or period: at any moment one may find oneself in another continent or another century ... it is a place where urban cares are left behind.

Steep paths past grottoes and cascades lead up through the bosco to

the lake. A boat lies rotting in the undergrowth, evoking scenes of holiday pastimes. Boating parties exploring the lakeside grottoes would have been drenched by the *giochi d'acqua* with which the boats were fitted. Their friends would enjoy the spectacle through holes pierced in the grotto ceilings, before losing themselves in the maze. Children might have swung out over the water on the iron swing that still stands by the water's edge. Lovers, doubtless, would be found everywhere, from the Mogul pavilion to the summer house with its mirror-covered walls and broderie garden dedicated to Flora.

   The boats no longer cross the lake, but otherwise little has changed: families still stand on the wrought-iron bridge to feed the turtles and enormous carp, and while they picnic beneath the weeping willow, oblivious lovers occupy the Chinese pagoda. Proof, as if it were needed, of how little human pleasures have changed over the years.

giardini botanici hanbury (la mortola)

NEAREST MAJOR TOWN Ventimiglia
MAIN FEATURES extensive botanical garden on a magnificent site overlooking the sea
PRE-BOOKING no
OWNER Università di Genova
ADDRESS Corso Montecarlo 43, 1-18039 Ventimiglia-Mortola Inferiore; tel.: +39 (0)184 229852/39507
LOCATION clearly signposted from the Ventimiglia exit off the A10

OPEN Monday, Tuesday, Thursday to Sunday, 31 March to 14 June, 10.00–17.00; 15 June to 29 September, 9.00–18.00; 30 September to 29 October, 10.00–17.00; 30 October to 30 March, 10.00–16.00
ADMISSION L8500, children L4500 (free under 6 years of age)
WHEELCHAIRS no
REFRESHMENTS yes
LAVATORIES yes

Sir Thomas Hanbury, an English businessman with a passionate interest in horticulture, bought La Mortola in 1867. The property comprised 45 hectares of rough ground and olive groves dropping 90 metres to the sea.

Sir Thomas and his brother Daniel, a pharmacologist with a particular interest in medicinal plants, wanted to create a botanical garden where exotics could be acclimatised to live naturally among indigenous species. A combination of climatic and geographical conditions created an ideal environment at La Mortola for this venture. The only problems were the long dry summers and the poor and rocky soil, but with the help of local labour these problems were overcome. Several underground reservoirs and irrigation channels were built, and the soil received intensive preparation. Even after this initial period the Hanburys continued to employ most of the adult population of the village to work in the house or garden. Sir Thomas became

an influential local figure. He built the school at Latte and the flower market in Ventimiglia.

In December 1868 Sir Thomas hired Ludwig Winter, a professional gardener. He worked at La Mortola for six years and imposed on the garden the structure that it retains to this day. The steep terraces were stocked with plants from nurseries throughout Europe. As the garden gained a reputation donations began to arrive and Sir Thomas soon built a collection of plants from temperate regions all over the world, eventually covering about 20 hectares. At the end of the century the director of Kew declared that La Mortola had 'no rival among the principal collections of living plants in the world'.

It is scarcely surprising that the gardens soon began to attract illustrious visitors. Queen Victoria, whose disapproval of gambling led her to spurn the hospitality of Monte Carlo, stayed with the Hanburys in 1882. Over the years other guests ranged from Benito Mussolini to Kuo Sung Tao, the first Chinese diplomat to be sent to England and France. To commemorate his visit he wrote the Chinese character 'fo', meaning happiness, on the arch at the entrance to the garden.

Sadly, Daniel Hanbury died in 1875 but Sir Thomas had 40 years more in which to work at extending and developing the garden before his death in 1907. His achievement is reflected in the third edition of *Hortus Mortolensis* printed in 1912. It was a catalogue of all the species in the garden and on this occasion it contained 5300 entries.

Cecil Hanbury and his wife Dorothy inherited the garden in 1920. Their interests were more aesthetic than botanical, and under their care various alterations were made to the planting and layout.

During the Second World War La Mortola became a minefield, and both the villa and garden were badly damaged. During the postwar years the whole question of restoring and maintaining the property became an insoluble problem. In 1960 Lady Dorothy handed it over to the State, thus initiating a long and complex period in its history that has almost proved to be fatal. Responsibility for the garden has passed between three principal bodies: the University of Genoa, the Sovraintendenza per i Beni Ambientali e Architettonici di Liguria and the Istituto Internazionale di Studi Liguri. Between 1980 and 1987 it had no owner at all. The gardeners were unpaid, and those that left were not replaced. Many of the plants that had survived neglect were then killed by the severe frosts of 1985 and 1986, leaving less than 1500 species. At one point the steps and terraces had been allowed to decay to such an extent that only one-third of the garden could be opened to the public; and only eight gardeners were employed to maintain it. However, since 1987 the Sovraintendenza and the university have worked hard to restore both the structure and the planting, and its future now looks fairly secure. A wave of concern about the plight of the gardens has resulted in the foundation of The Friends of the Hanbury Botanic Garden, an organisation that has an international membership united by the aim of returning the garden to its former splendour. (For details, write c/o The Royal Horticultural Society, PO Box 313, Vincent Square, London SW10 2PE, UK.)

The Victorian gateway built by Sir Thomas is still the main entrance to La Mortola. It frames a breathtaking view of the garden, with the sea creating a serene backdrop against which a mass of flowers and foliage drop steeply away at one's feet. Descending the labyrinth of winding paths through waves of scent and colour, it is hard to believe that little more than a century ago this was simply a barren hillside. La Mortola is still a remarkable collection, despite the occasional

liguria

evidence of neglect and frost damage. Even when the garden was at its nadir in the 1980s it was still worth visiting for the beauty of the site alone.

Immediately below the entrance is the small villa where Lady Dorothy passed the last years of her life. The house is still owned by the family. Almost at once the path divides, and one is faced with the first of many choices that have to be made in the course of the long descent. Each path leads between beds where plants from, for example, the Cape of Good Hope, Mexico, Ethiopia and Australia are mixed with indigenous species just as Hanbury intended. The skyline is punctuated with a curious mixture of trees. Native olive and cypress are interspersed with palm, pittosporum, eucalypt, exotic oak and Aleppo pine.

Sir Thomas' interests were not restricted to horticulture. He was a great collector, with a particular interest in classical antiquity. When restoration work on the villa is complete it will house the Hanbury sculpture collection. While the work is in progress the building is rather a bleak sight. However, there is a magnificent view over the lower garden to the sea from the terrace that Sir Thomas added to the south side of the villa.

The area in front of the villa was laid out as a parterre garden. Box and lavender hedges surrounded beds of medicinal herbs that were planted by Daniel. A few overgrown lavender bushes are all that remains of the layout.

It is in the area immediately surrounding the villa that Lady Dorothy's touch can most clearly be seen. There are the remains of a pergola, intended to be the longest in Europe, and a small, enclosed garden with brick paths that has a remarkably English feel to it. Hanbury's son and daughter-in-law also had flights of elegant, semicircular steps built between the terraces all over the garden, though many are now too dilapidated for use.

A cypress avenue leads down from the mausoleum of Sir Thomas and his wife towards the sea. Beyond the avenue the path is crossed by Via Giulia Augusta, the Roman road that cuts through the garden. The road runs along a deep trench, demonstrating the extent to which the soil level has risen in the past two millennia.

The citrus grove beyond the road represents a fascinating collection, which includes a specimen of the Shadock grapefruit that bears fruit weighing more than 1.3 kilograms.

NEAREST MAJOR TOWN Genoa
MAIN FEATURES Gothic Revival villa, nineteenth-century garden
PRE-BOOKING no
OWNER Comune di Arenzano
ADDRESS Via Sauli Pallavicino 39, Arenzano
LOCATION Arenzano is c. 22 kilometres west of Genoa towards Savona. The entrance to the villa is easily found from the car park in the centre of town
OPEN gardens 9.00–20.00, villa 9.00–12.30
ADMISSION free
WHEELCHAIRS yes
REFRESHMENTS no
LAVATORIES yes

Villa Negrotto has a considerably longer history than might be imagined from its present appearance. In its original form it was a simple watchtower known to have been standing in 1255. In 1558 the land was bought by Tobia Pallavicino who enlarged the tower into a castle. In 1825 Alessandro Pallavicino employed Ippolito Cremona, a Swiss engineer, to lay out the gardens, which included 10 kilometres of carriage drive. Alessandro's grand-daughter married Lazzaro Negrotto Cambiaso, who in 1880 had the castle entirely reconstructed in the Gothic Revival manner by the architect Rovelli. The original watchtower was rebuilt with a huge new loggia. The fine 'Liberty'-style greenhouse was built by Lamberto Cusani for the Marchesa Matilda Negrotto-Cambiaso Giustiniani.

The estate was opened to the public for the first time in 1985 when it came into the ownership of the Comune di Arenzano, whose offices it now houses.

This garden provides an interesting contrast with the neo-classical garden of Villa Durazzo Pallavicini, laid out only a few years later (page 62). It cannot be considered as representative of any particular

period, but simply as containing all the features that brought pleasure to the hearts of Alessandro Pallavicino and his successors.

The entrance avenue of ilex soon gives way to well-grown stands of the palms that appear in every corner of the grounds. On the left lies open parkland while on the right a stream descends through the woods via pools and cascades. At the head of the avenue, in front of the villa, is a pool decorated with the traditional Ligurian mosaic and occupied by turtles (further proof of the mildness of the climate).

Immediately behind the villa is the upper terrace linked to the *piano nobile* by a bridge. Two large grottoes lie beneath this. The spirit of their (now defunct) *giochi d'acqua* appears to have passed into the plumbing of the neighbouring lavatories. A tunnel between the grottoes ascends to the upper terrace with its fishpond and lawn.

To the right a path leads to a castellated 'curtain wall'. On arrival this turns out to be no more than the thickness of a brick and serves to disguise a group of greenhouses below. This fanciful illusion is of a type more common to Northern Europe (one example being William Kent's castellated farmhouse at Stowe, Buckinghamshire).

The path continues to a large parterre arranged around a single central palm, the whole bed being surrounded by festoons and swags of roses. Over to the left stands Cusani's greenhouse, splendidly assertive against its dramatic mountain background.

Turning right one returns to the front of the villa. Setting off once again to the left of it one reaches the balustraded terrace that overlooks the park. It runs beneath the retaining wall of the upper terrace with its machicolated watchtowers and leads eventually to the mock-gothic servants quarters and stables. From here one can enter the park, whose main feature is undoubtedly the duck pond filled with ornamental waterfowl. Their eggs are much appreciated by the locals.

veneto

regional introduction

The Veneto runs from the marshes and lagoons of Venice to the wooded hills around Verona. During the fifteenth century the rich and noble families of Venice began to reject trade as a form of investment and turned to the agricultural land of the Veneto as an alternative. Three centuries of relative peace and prosperity followed. During the seventeenth and eighteenth centuries the building of villas in the Veneto became a competitive passion, best illustrated by those along the Brenta canal, each one bigger and better than the last. Sadly, little remains of the gardens that surrounded them. Villa Pisani is one of the few exceptions, however. In 1797, Napoleon put an end to the Venetian Republic, and to the luxurious lifestyle that went with it. Many gardens were destroyed in the turbulent years that followed.

Despite widely differing terrain, the gardens of the Veneto do not vary greatly in style. Unlike the Romans, the Venetians were not attracted by complex architectural features. Consequently, even the gardens built on sloping sites, such as Barbarigo, tended to adhere to a relatively simple design. Sadly, the fact that many of them were made up of such ephemeral things as *berceaux*, pergolas and parterres means that they have disappeared without trace. Other gardens were victims to the fashion for French designs, which took hold particularly early in the low-lying areas of the Veneto.

NEAREST MAJOR TOWN Verona

MAIN FEATURES seventeenth-century villa and garden in a rural setting, early example of *broderie* parterres

PRE-BOOKING yes

OWNER Signore Ottavio Arvedi

ADDRESS loc. Cuzzano, I-37023 Grezzana; tel. +39 (0)45 907045

LOCATION Cuzzano is c. 11 kilometres north of Verona. From Verona follow signs for the SS11 to Vicenza, but on the outskirts of Verona there will be signs for Grezzana. Take the turning for Grezzana centro. The villa is on hillside above the road. Note that although they appear very close on the map, allow plenty of time to go cross-country between Villa Allegri and Villa Rizzardi

OPEN strictly by appointment

ADMISSION free

WHEELCHAIRS no

REFRESHMENTS no

LAVATORIES no

Villa Allegri was built in 1656 for Giovanni Battista Allegri. The architect, Giovanni Battista Bianchi, built it on the site of an existing house, which had been the family's home since 1500.

The *parterre de broderie* below the villa is thought to date from the end of the seventeenth century. Parterre gardens were generally still being laid out in the traditional manner in Italy at this time. It was not until the eighteenth century that the French fashion for *broderie* began to take the place of square parterres divided by gravel paths. Villa Allegri is remarkable not only as an unusually early example of the French influence on Italian garden design, but also because its elaborate layout has survived intact for nearly 300 years.

In 1824 the villa was bought by Giovanni Antonio Arvedi, and it remains in the family's hands to this day. The garden is unchanged, although the *limonaia* that once stood along the left wall was demolished during the nineteenth century. A swimming pool has now taken

its place, and traces of the frescoed stucco that decorated the original building cling to the wall behind the pool.

The villa is a working farm set in the midst of a beautiful agricultural landscape. The hill rising steeply behind the house is planted with olives, giving way to oak and hornbeam. The building is flanked by two square dovecotes, to which it is linked by terraces extending from the *piano nobile*.

The drive once extended in a straight line below the villa. During the last century its course was altered to create the informal curve that now leads up from the gatehouse. The result of the new layout is an unusual perspective by which the villa is seen across a charming mixture of geometrical parterre beds, topiary, fruit trees and fields. To left and right persimmons form a wide, informal avenue made particularly striking late in the year by their golden fruit. Vines grow between the trees, and box hedges and clipped cypress stand to either side of the drive.

The drive leads below the retaining wall of the terrace, and into a courtyard behind the villa. The courtyard is similar to the lower garden in that it is both practical and delightfully ornamental. Flanked by stables and outhouses, it is completed by the ornate façade of the family chapel, which is still used every Sunday. It stands opposite the villa, at the top of two flights of balustraded steps, and is said to have been built to commemorate San Carlo Borommeo's visit in 1542. Apparently the cardinal stopped at Cuzzano on his way to the Council of Trent, which suggests that the chapel may predate the villa. The niches in the retaining wall below the building once held statues. However, they are supposed to have been destroyed by Arvedi's daughter, Lucidalba. She had recently taken holy orders and was offended by the fact that the pagan figures stood so close to the chapel.

veneto

An ideal view of the garden is from the balcony that runs along the *piano nobile*. The survival of the *parterre de broderie* bears witness to years of dedicated care by the Arvedi. Low box hedges create a swirling and complex design punctuated by large cones of clipped box. The edge of the garden is decorated with lemons in pots. Earlier in this century roses were planted among the *broderie* beds. However, the garden has been restored to its original form by the present owner, and it is beautifully maintained by only two gardeners.

(villa donà delle rosa)

NEAREST MAJOR TOWN Padua
MAIN FEATURES late seventeenth-century garden in rural setting, rabbit island
PRE-BOOKING no
OWNER Count Pizzoni Ardemani
ADDRESS I-35030 Valsanzibio di Galzignano
LOCATION Valsanzibio is c. 18 kilometres south of Padua. Follow signs for the SS16 to Monselice from the centre of Padua. After

c. 15 kilometres turn off for Battaglia Terme; drive through the town and cross the railway. Valsanzibio is signposted left almost immediately. The villa is signposted from the village
OPEN I March to 30 November, 9.00–12.00, 14.00–dusk; closed Sunday mornings/public holidays
ADMISSION L9500, children L6500
WHEELCHAIRS no
REFRESHMENTS no
LAVATORIES no

The Barbarigo was an illustrious Venetian family who had bought some of the marshy land near Valsanzibio. In 1631, when exiled to the country by an outbreak of plague in Venice, they planned a new villa, but it was not till 1669 that Antonio Barbarigo, who was to become Procurator of San Marco, gave orders for building work to begin. The architect is unknown.

The garden evolved over many decades. Documents preserved in the Museo Correr in Venice record its progress over the years. A map of 1678 shows the work well advanced, but by no means complete. In the same year payment was made for iron supports for the statues. In 1694 a building was demolished to make way for a further extension to the layout. In 1717, the Barbarigo bought additional land, thus securing rights over the little stream and drainage canal that were to feed the pools and fountains of the garden.

Villa Barbarigo soon became famous for its magnificent flower gar-

veneto

den. During the seventeenth century the green garden of the early Renaissance had been largely abandoned in Italy. The Barbarigo were evidently enthralled by the new fashion for rare plants, some imported from as far afield as India and the Americas. Paolo Bartolomeo Clarici, whose *Istoria e coltura delle piante* was published in Venice in 1726, was particularly impressed by the double stocks. He listed 233 different plants in the garden and 226 different kinds of fruit.

During the Second World War the villa narrowly escaped destruction when the avenue above it was bombed. The trees have been replanted by the present owners.

The property eventually passed out of Barbarigo hands to the Donà delle Rose. It now belongs to the Pizzoni Ardemani.

Before entering the garden it is worth walking the few yards down the road to the watergate. It is said that the pool that lies between the gate and the road was once a part of the web of canals that covered this area and linked Valsanzibio to Venice. If this was the case, the Barbarigo's guests would have seen the garden for the first time from the level of the watergate, and it is right that one should share their experience. It may be that the gate was never used, and that it was designed simply for the enjoyment of passers-by who could admire the pools and cascades that descend the gentle slope behind it. The creation of views through the boundary wall dates from the fifteenth century in the Veneto, and should not be confused with the French fashion for *clairvoyées*.

The watergate is dedicated entirely to the terra firma sport of hunting. Diana stands on the broken arch of the pediment with her dogs. The entire structure is decorated with bas-reliefs of game that has been caught and is already neatly hung: deer, bear, fox, hare and wild boar are all accurately portrayed alongside the paraphernalia of the chase. The contemporary visitor enters the garden through the base of an unfinished tower in the boundary wall and emerges in an area of eighteenth-century woodland. The garden is contained in a natural amphitheatre in the Euganean hills and the two intersecting vistas that form its core are designed to lead the eye up to the wooded slopes that enclose the site on all sides. Consequently, one is always aware of the magnificence of its setting.

The first vista is created by the two pools that lie on the gentle slope above the watergate. The first is presided over by two enormous bearded sea gods who lie against its rough retaining wall. The angle of the slope is such that the other pool is all but invisible from the watergate. Twelve-foot box hedges enclose the area on both sides. Between the pools four delightfully mischievous putti dangle their feet in their own circular pond.

The garden's second axis crosses the first immediately above the pools. It consists of a *tapis vert* that runs the length of the site. A gardener with an enormously long wooden ladder and a plumb line clips the huge box hedges that flank the *tapis vert* and serve to frame the villa which stands at its far end. The vista is extended by means of a cypress avenue cutting through the trees on the slope above the villa.

At the far end of the *tapis vert* steps lead up to the bright parterres and beautiful topiary of the private garden in front of the villa. Each step is inscribed with verses describing the garden as a kind of private paradise: sun and moon shine brightly, Mars lays down his weapons, death is powerless and tears have no place. The images are those of an earlier period, far removed from the unsettled universe that dominated the baroque imagination and infiltrated the gardens of the age.

A massive statue of Father Time, bent beneath the weight of his load, stands in a clearing in the *bosco* between the stables and watergate. He was undoubtedly part of a wider symbolic theme now largely lost to the modern imagination.

One of the most delightful features of the garden is the rabbit island in a clearing in the *bosco*. It is encircled by a moat and can only be reached by a wooden drawbridge. Worn statues of rabbits stand at the water's edge, and at the centre of the island there is a rustic stone tower supporting an ornate aviary. The white doves that inhabit it are oblivious of a realistic stone hawk that hovers over them, but their peace, and that of this delightful garden, is occasionally shattered by the arrival of the owner's passionately friendly Airedales.

NEAREST MAJOR TOWN Padua

MAIN FEATURES unique gothic castle with extensive sixteenth- and early nineteenth-century gardens

PRE-BOOKING no

OWNER dalla Francesca family

ADDRESS I-35041 Battaglia Terme; tel.: +39 (0)49 526541

LOCATION Battaglia Terme is c. 16 kilometres south-west of Padua. From Padua take the A13 towards Ferrara, exiting at Terme Euganée. Catajo is on the SS16 to Battaglia. This gate is locked, so go into Battaglia, turning right over the canal. Take the first turning right below the embankment road (ignoring the sign saying private road). The road leads between fields and houses. Turn right again on to dirt track leading towards the castle

OPEN 1 March to 30 November, Tuesday and Sunday, 14.30–21.00; other days by appointment only

ADMISSION L10,000

WHEELCHAIRS no

REFRESHMENTS no

LAVATORIES no

The extraordinary collection of buildings that make up the Castello del Catajo date from 1570. However, their gothic style makes them an anomaly in Italian architecture of the sixteenth century.

Pius Aeneas degli Olbizzi employed Andrea della Valle to design the main building. It was built on the site of an existing family villa, already known as Catajo after the hill on which it was built. Edith Wharton suggests that the design was based on the plans brought back by Marco Polo of a castle in Tartary. Whatever the source of his inspiration, della Valle certainly created a fitting home for Olbizzi who was a distinguished man-at-arms in the Venetian army. Almost stranger than the design itself is the fact that it took only three years to build.

Olbizzi's nephew, Pius Aeneas II, inherited Catajo in 1648. He was impassioned about it and spent the next 18 years extending the build-

veneto

ing and laying out magnificent gardens. However, he never employed an architect, believing that he was the only person capable of truly understanding the site. Tommaso was the last of the Olbizzi, and when he died at the beginning of the nineteenth century he left Catajo to the Duke of Modena. It then passed to the Habsburg family who extended it, made it a summer residence, and took the Olbizzi collection of paintings and sculptures with them to Vienna.

veneto

The Habsburgs sold the castle to the dalla Francesca family. The three dalla Francesca sisters, who had an unfortunate reputation for miserliness, set up a business growing and drying tobacco. None were married, and when the last sister died in 1986 the property was inherited by three different families.

The creation of the gardens cannot have been an easy task. The castle was built against a steep hill, and the grounds were bound on one

veneto

side by the Brenta Canal. Despite these difficulties Pius Aeneas II built an extraordinary number of different gardens. The site dictated that many should be terraces and hanging gardens. During the nineteenth century, his gardens above the Brenta were compared with the Hanging Gardens of Babylon. Additional terraces were wedged between the castle walls and the hill behind it. Fountains, *giochi d'acqua*, courtyards, ramps and passages added to the fascination of the eccentric layout.

Sadly, we have only seen a fraction of all that Catajo has to offer, being allowed only in the garden that lies on the level ground below the castle's south wall. This part of the garden was originally laid out around two balustraded fishponds, decorated with oranges in pots. According to a contemporary description pergolas surrounded the garden, clematis and jasmine hung in swags from the retaining wall below the drive, and there was a bosco planted with elm and a maze.

The existing garden bears little resemblance to Pius Aeneas' seventeenth-century creation. The layout, probably designed for Tommaso, dates from the early nineteenth century. Much as one dislikes linking neglect with the idea of romance in a garden, it cannot be denied that the passage of years has turned this into a wild and romantic place, despite the struggles of the gardener employed to maintain it.

A long walk, lined from end to end with pots of citrus fruit and flowering geranium, runs the width of the garden. The greenhouses, which are concealed from the drive by a neo-gothic façade, stand at one end. At the other, steps lead up to the raised drive immediately in front of the castle's main entrance. The jasmine and clematis of the seventeenth century have been ousted by climbing roses.

The rest of the garden is divided between a lake, which may have

veneto

replaced the fishponds of the earlier layout, and a wooded area. The magnificent magnolias that surround the lake were planted by Tommaso in 1803. Low box hedges stand to either side of the path that runs by the water's edge. At the far end of the lake weeping willows screen a view of the castle across the water. The wood that covers the rest of the site is divided by a series of parallel avenues, walks and beech tunnels. The principal avenue leads to a cenotaph, erected by Tommaso in memory of his wife. The area between the avenue and the lake was once a web of little paths, but they are now for the most part impassable. However, determined explorers may find the swimming pool, which must date from the beginning of this century, and the derelict bathing hut. The pool can only be reached by walking through the remains of the small maze, which no doubt guaranteed the privacy of the bathers.

NEAREST MAJOR TOWN Verona
MAIN FEATURES delightful sixteenth-century garden
PRE-BOOKING no
OWNER Conte Giusti del Giardino
ADDRESS Via Giusti 2, I-37129 Verona; tel.: +39 (0)45 8034029

LOCATION follow signs for Giardino Giusti from the centre of town
OPEN dawn to dusk; may be closed Monday
ADMISSION L7000 (garden only)
WHEELCHAIRS yes, in lower garden
REFRESHMENTS no
LAVATORIES yes

The Giusti was originally a Tuscan family that came to Verona at the beginning of the fifteenth century and bought property beneath the hill of San Zeno, just beyond the city boundaries. Nobody knows whether their full title of Giusti del Giardino acted as a self-fulfilling prophecy or whether, more probably, it dates from the creation of the garden that was to become famous all over Europe.

Count Agostino Giusti – a powerful figure in the political and cultural life of Verona – had the gardens laid out sometime between 1565 and 1580. The architect is unknown and none of the original plans survive. Over the centuries, however, many visitors have depicted and described the garden, which was open to the public from its creation. Johann Christoph Volkamer's engraving of 1714 shows a pool in the south-eastern section of the lower garden rather like the one at Villa Lante (page 314) with an island linked to the garden by a bridge. A statue of Venus, thought to have been by Alessandro Vittoria, stood at the island's centre. This delightful feature survived at least until the nineteenth century, as it is included in the 1830 official records.

During Agostino's lifetime the garden was often used as a setting for plays and concerts. In 1581 Torquato Tasso's *Aminta* was staged here

for the third time. It is said that the mouth of the grotesque mask on the cliff face was made to spit fire for the occasion, and strange music issued from one of the grottoes.

In 1611 the English traveller Thomas Coryate visited 'Count Augustus Justus' and was shown round the garden. He described it as 'a passing delectable place of solace, beautified with many curious knots, fruits of divers sorts and two rowes of lofty cypresse trees, three and thirty in ranke'.

In 1615 Agostino died and his son Giovan Giacomo Giusti inherited the property. In 1621 he was granted permission to convey water to the garden from a nearby stream and he built additional fountains of a more complex design and installed various *giochi d'acqua*. Previously, rainwater collected in a large underground cistern beneath a well in the upper garden had been the sole water supply.

The garden belongs to the Giusti to this day. However, continuity of ownership – which has so often protected the original layout of a garden – has not been entirely effective in this case. When Georgina Masson saw it she complained of the inappropriate landscaping of the slope below the cliff.

The garden is built on two levels linked by a spiral staircase. The lower garden lies on the same level as the villa and is enclosed on three sides by walls made up in part by the remains of the city's fortifications. A sheer cliff face forms the northern boundary. The upper garden lies on a narrow shelf at the top of the cliff.

A high wall separates the garden from the arcaded entrance of the palazzo. A wrought-iron gate let into the centre of the wall allows passers-by to enjoy a glimpse of the garden from the street. The gate is on axis with the famous cypress avenue that has provoked the wonder of successive generations of visitors. The massive trees create striped shadows, seeming to reflect the lines of the steps that link the avenue to the base of the cliff. There is a hideous mask hewn out of the rough face of the cliff above the steps. Its teeth are bared in fury at the unsuspecting visitors who lean over the balustrade of the belvedere built above its head. Its design is reminiscent of the curious fireplaces at Villa della Torre Cazzola and of the grotto in the Sacro Bosco in Bomarzo (pages 118 and 282).

Volkamer's print suggests that the garden may originally have been laid out as a series of garden rooms to either side of the avenue. Perhaps it was on account of their Tuscan origins that the Giusti chose a design that had so much more in common with the gardens of Central Italy than with those of the Veneto. To the east this layout has been preserved. A row of cypresses acts as a screen, dividing the garden in two. The first 'room' is filled with green parterres arranged around a simple fountain where water and weeds combine to delightful effect. Female statues stand among the cypresses that bound the garden on all sides. Many of the Roman tombstones collected by Agostino and Gian Giacomo Giusti still stand in this part of the garden.

In his diary of 1736 President de Brosses records a nasty experience in the gardens: 'I got lost in a maze, and I was an hour wandering in the blazing sun, and would have still been there, had I not been taken out by one of the people of the place'. The maze still stands behind the cypress screen, just as it does in Volkamer's print of 1714. It was redesigned by Luigi Trezza in 1786.

The left-hand portion of the lower garden is also divided by cypresses. They were planted recently to restore the original layout; they are still too small to create a screen and consequently the sweep

sweep of the box parterres that climb the slope below the cliff can be enjoyed from the bottom of the garden. The beds are divided by gravel paths decorated with lemons in pots. Each is made of a complex combination of interlocking shapes, rather like the parts of a puzzle. The pale statues that grace the parterres stand out against the rich greens of cypress and box.

The ancient city wall creates the boundary of this side of the garden. It used to serve as the rear wall of the *limonaia*, which was decorated with statues of Ceres, Bacchus and Venus by Lorenzo Muttoni. These still stand in their original positions along the wall.

The steps at the end of the avenue mark the transition between the formal and the wild sections of the garden. Terraces originally extended to either side of them, and were planted with fig, orange, lemon and apricot.

A classical portal forms the entrance to the grotto at the top of the steps. Little remains however of its fabulous interior. The walls were once covered with conch shells, coral, mother-of-pearl, painted glass and pebbles, and some of the decoration can still be seen on the ceiling. Landscapes painted in the niches on the walls to right and left seemed to transform the grotto into an open loggia. Traces of the painted stucco cling to the wall just inside the entrance. A pair of mirrors used to be set in the far wall, creating the illusion that another, identical garden lay beyond.

Four other grottoes were let into the cliff at different levels. There was one above the maze, built in such a way that it amplified and distorted sound. Another, which can still be seen at the foot of the tower that links the lower and upper gardens, served as the family chapel.

A winding path leads up the wooded slope, passing at one point through a pergola and at another through a charming open loggia, to emerge eventually at the foot of the tower built against the cliff face. The worn spiral staircase in the tower is the only link between the two levels of the garden.

Rare vegetables and scented herbs were once planted on the undulating site of the upper garden. A circular temple, demolished in 1920, stood to the east, and the Palazzina di Venere (Little Palace of Venus) formed its boundary to the west. From the belvedere there is a magnificent view down the avenue and across Verona.

veneto

NEAREST MAJOR TOWN Padua
MAIN FEATURES beautifully maintained, large, sixteenth-century garden
PRE-BOOKING yes
OWNER Conte Vettore Marcello
ADDRESS loc. Levada, I-35017 Piombino Dese; tel.: +39 (0)49 9350340
LOCATION from Padua take the SS307 for Castelfranco. After c. 25 kilometres turn right in Resana for Levada. The villa lies unmistakably on the left just through Levada
OPEN April to October, organised groups only by arrangement
ADMISSION free
WHEELCHAIRS yes
REFRESHMENTS no
LAVATORIES no

Villa Marcello was built for the family of the same name in 1580. All the documents concerning its early history were destroyed during the Second World War. During the nineteenth century additions were made to the back of the main building, and the arcades were built at the front. During the First World War the villa was commandeered by the Germans as a base. Apart from this brief interlude it has been in the hands of the Marcello since it was built.

The sixteenth-century garden is behind the villa and consists of a *bosco*, canal and long, rectangular pool. The *bosco* is made up of beech, plane and poplar planted in a series of long walks and avenues. Sixteenth-century Venetian statues stand in the dappled shade at the end of each avenue. Originally, the area between the avenues was planted with fruit trees. A sixteenth-century dovecote stands at the far end of the central avenue, on axis with the villa. It is a substantial building of several storeys. During the First World War it housed carrier pigeons, and the room below the tower was the office from where they were despatched. After the war the building was used for housing silkworms.

veneto

The rear wall of the villa is decorated with a series of charming statues depicting monkey musicians. The monkeys are only just over a foot high and stand on a series of pillars. There are seven of them in all, one on the cymbals, another playing a concertina and the others joining in with the violin, tambourine, pan-pipes and banjo. The conductor stands at the centre with baton raised. The pool lies directly behind the villa, creating a striking perspective from the *piano nobile*. It is flanked by gnarled beech tunnels, and at the far end the eye is stopped by a simple brick wall ornamented with putti. Closer examination reveals that they are holding sheaves of corn, flowers and grapes. There is a curious collection of statues standing along the boundary wall of the garden. A bridled Venetian lion represents Venice conquered by the Austrians. It is curious that this should have been allowed to survive after the liberation of the Veneto.

The pool is fed by a canal that leads in from the fields. It was originally dug to get the clay needed to make bricks when building the villa. When its practical use was over, it was made into one of the decorative features of the garden. It is shaded by trees, and a series of sixteenth-century Venetian dwarves stand along its banks. Such statues are common in the Veneto, but these seem unusually grotesque.

In front of the villa is a formal garden laid out in the Italian manner. Large, green parterres divided by gravel walks are arranged around a central fountain. These were planted after the Second World War, replacing a nineteenth-century layout. The paths winding through the trees to either side of the parterres are its only relic. In one of the trees there is a magnificent tree house, though it is not an original feature.

veneto

NEAREST MAJOR TOWN Padua
MAIN FEATURES unusual late
eighteenth-century public garden
PRE-BOOKING no
OWNER Comune di Padova
ADDRESS Padua
LOCATION Prato della Valle is by the
Oratorio di San Giorgio in the centre

of town. Follow signs to San Giorgio.
Parking is off Viale Carducci/Via 58
Fanteria
OPEN free
ADMISSION free
WHEELCHAIRS yes
REFRESHMENTS no
LAVATORIES no

Prato della Valle was the name given to a field in the middle of Padua. It was too boggy for permanent buildings and was plagued by annual flooding. The Romans used it as a burial ground, and later it was a site for fairs and markets.

When Andrea Memmo became Governor of Padua in 1775, he recognised the political advantage to be gained by solving the age-old problem of the Prato. The subject was topical at the time, following a particularly severe flood. Memmo's motives were not purely political. He had a genuine desire to create something that would bring pleasure to the citizens of the city and he wanted to give them a garden so unusual that visitors would be drawn from all over Europe to see it, the visitors providing the city with a new source of income. Memmo extended the idea of mixing pleasure and commerce by suggesting that there should be shops in the garden.

Domenico Cerato was commissioned to help Memmo by drawing up the plans for the project. Between them they created a striking design that has been preserved by the Civic Museum in Padua. Their idea was to dig an oval canal in the centre of the site, using the earth from the excavation to make a raised island. The canal was to be fed

veneto

EVGENIO

by water drained off the rest of the field. It was an ingenious idea, providing a neat solution both to the problem of flooding and to the need for form and a focus for the irregular site.

Cerato's plan and the structure of the island today are identical in all but two respects. A portico was to be built around the perimeter of the island to house the shops. Part of it was to be a permanent structure supported by stone columns, and the rest was to be made of wood painted to look like marble. In the event, the excessive cost of draining the area and the scepticism of local tradesmen combined to persuade Memmo to drop the portico from the plans. The failure of the commercial aspect of the plan was a severe blow for him. It altered the garden's place in the life of the city, cutting it off from daily life and turning it into a place reserved only for pleasure and repose.

The site of four structures described as *berceaux* was marked on the original plans. Cerato's notes stipulate that these should be Chinese in appearance, and decorated with a black-and-white pattern. An engraving of 1786 by Francesco Piranesi shows the *berceaux* in place – looking more like striped tents.

Cerato's plan shows the canal lined, as it is today, by innumerable statues. Executed by local artists and outsiders, the statues were all donations. The first to be produced depicted the Roman Republican statesman Cicero. This outraged the citizens of Padua, who felt that a Roman, however worthy, could not be given a place of honour in their city. Following this incident it was announced that the statues had to represent famous people or heroes linked to the city or its university. Curiously, no saints were allowed. Seventy-eight figures were produced in all over about 60 years.

The urban designers of this century have made no concessions to the

Prato della Valle, using its perimeter as a massive roundabout. However, the raised island and canal flanked by statues are still instantly recognisable amid the cars.

Four bridges span the canal and lead to the broad walks that intersect the island and meet at its centre. Impressive bishops with copes and mitres preside over two of the bridges, stretching out their hands in benediction. The stone benches that stand around the central 'piazza' (so named by Cerato) and the urns on pedestals that decorate the walks were all included in the original plan.

The plane trees were planted during the nineteenth century. Overcrowding and disease detract from their beauty and, far from adorning the site, they obscure the bold lines of Cerato's design.

The statues are a marvellous sight. Most were executed by artists whose identities have been lost. However, one statue is attributed to Antonio Canova. Each statue stands on a pedestal inscribed in Latin with the name and credentials of the subject.

NEAREST MAJOR TOWN Verona
MAIN FEATURES sixteenth-century villa and garden in classical Roman style in the Valpolicella
PRE-BOOKING yes
OWNER Dr Gianantonio Cazzola
ADDRESS I-37022 Fumane;
tel.: +39 (0)45 912104/8033204
LOCATION Fumane is c. 22 kilometres north-west of Verona. Take the SS12 for Trento from Verona, turning off at Parona after c. 6 kilometres. Turn off towards Negrar and then follow signs for Fumane. The villa is on the far side of the village and is recognised by the chapel's crenellated bell tower. The entrance is a dirt track beyond the boundary wall leading to the farmyard
OPEN April to September: Saturday, 15.00–19.00; Sunday to Friday by appointment
ADMISSION L6000
WHEELCHAIRS no
REFRESHMENTS no
LAVATORIES no

Giulio della Torre came into possession of the land on which the villa is built through his marriage in 1504. Although it is not known exactly when building work began, it has been established that it was not finished by the time of his death in 1547. However, a map of 1562 shows the villa complete.

Della Torre was a classical scholar and it was fitting that his home should imitate the Roman villas that fired his imagination. Consequently, the house is built around a colonnaded peristyle that once enclosed a garden. After Giulio's death the property passed to his son, Girolamo, and from him to Marcantonio della Torre. During Marcantonio's lifetime it became a meeting place for his cultured and influential friends. It is to this era that we owe the delightful verses of the Venetian poet Veronica Franco. Her poems pay tribute not only to the garden, but also to the gardener who tended it. Very little documen-

tary evidence has survived about the villa's early history. The architect
has never been finally established, although it is generally attributed to
Giulio Romano. The fireplaces inside the villa, set in the gaping jaws
of grotesque masks, seem to correspond with Romano's bizarre sense
of humour. Cristoforo Sorte is said to have been responsible for the
complex system by which water was brought to the garden from afar,
and which has recently been restored by the owners.

The villa stands against the side of a steep hill in the Valpolicella. Its
isolated position and the unsettled times explain the Della Torre's decision to enclose their garden with a high boundary wall. The original
entrance was at the bottom of the lower garden. Lawns, intersected by
four paths and decorated with a central fountain, once filled the space
now taken up by a vineyard. Today, one enters the garden at the level
of the terrace in front of the villa. It is linked to the lower garden by
four flights of steps, under which there is a grotto. A striking oblong
pool spanned by a triple-arched bridge stands at the centre of the terrace. The aviary on the far wall would once have been full of songbirds,
just as the pool was full of fish.

Like the villas of ancient Rome, Villa della Torre had a garden laid
out on a single axis. The climax of its four-part design was created by
the courtyard garden in the colonnaded peristyle of the house. By
standing at the centre of the courtyard one could look across the bridge
that spanned the pool, down the path that divided the lower garden
and through the entrance at its far end. Behind the villa the vista was
extended by an avenue that climbed the slope beyond the boundaries
of the enclosed garden.

The villa's principal rooms open into the colonnades that surround
the courtyard. When the doors were open, the courtyard would have

served simply as another room in the house. This fusion between house and garden was also inspired by Roman designs.

In architectural terms, the courtyard represents a somewhat eccentric interpretation of the original. To appreciate the effect that Giulio wished to achieve, one must imagine the space filled with magnificent pots of orange and lemon, and alive with the sound of the water that ran from the fountain and the grotesques either side of the doors. The niches under the shady colonnades are now empty, but they once held the statues of pagan figures. At night the walls would have leapt with the shadows thrown by burning torches in the sconces on the walls.

If the courtyard is to be seen as a Roman garden, the area behind the villa resembles a *hortus conclusus*. It is sheltered by high walls, and much of the space is taken up by cherry, apple, pear and persimmon. A swing hangs from one of the trees, and rough grass and wild flowers grow between them. A flight of steps runs up the central axis to a low terrace that bounds the garden on all sides. One side of the terrace is given up to a bowling alley, and the family chapel stands in the opposite corner. The bell tower is decorated with curious brick battlements, matching those that crown the boundary wall of the terrace in front of the villa. The garden is full of the sound of birdsong and the bleating of the sheep that scramble about on the hillside above.

NEAREST MAJOR TOWN Padua
MAIN FEATURES large eighteenth-century garden in the French manner with maze and moated coffee house
PRE-BOOKING no
OWNER the State
ADDRESS Via A Pisani, 1-630039 Strà; tel.: +39 (0)49 9800590
LOCATION Strà is c. 8 kilometres east of Padua. Leave Padua on the SS11 for Venice. The villa and car park are on the left just beyond Strà
OPEN Tuesday to Sunday, 9.00–13.30
ADMISSION L8000, children free
WHEELCHAIRS yes
REFRESHMENTS no
LAVATORIES yes

Alvise Pisani was the Venetian ambassador to Paris between 1699 and 1704, and Louis XIV was godfather to his son. In 1711, he became Procurator of San Marco in Venice, and in 1735 was elected Doge. It is fitting that the villa designed for him by Francesco Maria Preti should be the largest and most elaborate on the Brenta.

For almost 20 years Alvise and his brother Almoro had been planning to demolish the simple sixteenth-century family residence and replace it with something more elaborate. Girolamo Frigimelica had been commissioned to draw up plans for a new villa and garden in 1719. The existing building was duly demolished in 1720; Frigimelica's replacement was started by 1735 and continued by Francesco Preti. It was completed by 1756. However, his design for the gardens was retained, and when the villa was built in 1735 it had to be fitted into the space that Frigimelica had originally left for it.

Villa Pisani stayed in the family till 1807 when Napoleon ordered that it should be bought by the Kingdom of Italy. He spent one night there himself, and then presented it to his viceroy, Eugene de Beauharnais, thus initiating its role in public life.

veneto

During the reorganisation that followed the Napoleonic period Austria was granted possession of the Veneto. For the first 30 years of Austrian rule the villa and its grounds were completely neglected. However, in 1849 it became a military hospital, and some restoration work was initiated. In 1882 it was declared a national monument.

During the early years of this century the villa was privately managed with the aid of a State subsidy, but after the Second World War it reverted to State ownership. Lack of staff and funding reduced the building and its grounds to such a critical condition that it had to be closed in 1979. Thankfully, restoration work is now underway. However, Frigimelica's splendid garden is badly scarred by more than a century of neglect.

As they alighted from their boat, Alvise's visitors could have looked through the massive portico of the villa and along the central perspective of the garden. Today the north–south perspective is created by a sheet of water along the length of the garden. Originally, the entire space was filled with *parterres de broderie*, but in 1911 they were torn out for the pool, which was then used for testing naval-scale models. At the time this was undoubtedly an act of vandalism. However, one cannot fail to appreciate the effect of the still water stretching away from the villa and the reflection of the beautiful façade of Frigimelica's stable block that has survived to create a focus for the central axis of the garden. As an habitué of the French court, Pisani would have been familiar with the work of the garden designer André Le Nôtre. He may have encouraged Frigimelica to adopt some of the Frenchman's ideas, which were becoming increasingly fashionable in Italy at that time. Whether influenced by Le Nôtre, Frigimelica's decision to base his design around a series of avenues was certainly appropriate to the flat site.

The three sections that made up the original garden still form the basis of its layout. To either side of the parterres Frigimelica planted areas of *bosco* intersected by avenues. The avenues created vistas along the length of the garden. Additional avenues radiated from the vertical axis and were aligned to lead the eye across the parterres and through the trees beyond. The doors and windows that pierce the boundary wall allowed the vistas to extend to the countryside beyond.

It is in the right-hand portion of the garden that the original design is best seen. The magnificent maze is at the end of a long lime avenue. Its entrance is flanked by two laughing putti, witnesses to the desperation of many an illustrious guest lost among the 2-metre hedges within. Pisani could watch their efforts from the delightful tower at the centre of the maze, which he would have climbed by means of the ornate spiral staircase that encircles it. The statue of Minerva crowning the tower may be an allusion to the difficulty of attaining wisdom.

Frigimelica's curious hexagonal arch is in the middle of the *bosco* at the centre of six radiating avenues. Worn stone steps spiral up through the building and emerge on a balustraded terrace. From this vantage point one can look down the avenues in all directions. However, the trees have reached such a height that the view of the garden may not be as comprehensive as Frigimelica intended. The *limonaie* run away from the arch to left and right. There was a time when they sheltered 66 varieties of citrus tree. When the villa belonged to the Pisani as many as 20,000 lemons were sold each year. Until the mid-nineteenth century, prize-winning camellias continued to be grown in the hot houses at the villa.

Frigimelica's coffee house stands on a mound that used to be planted with hedges clipped as flights of steps. During the nineteenth century the hedges were lost, tall trees were planted around the site and the moat dug as part of a new drainage system.

The *bosco* to the left of the villa was originally divided into five distinct areas by a series of avenues. Each area was slightly different: one had a lawn with a central statue, another was characterised by box hedges and the one furthest from the villa was filled with paths that wound through the trees to a little mound. Most of this part of the garden was destroyed during the nineteenth century. Here, as elsewhere in the garden, the trees are in a poor and untended state.

The garden is now being painstakingly restored by the state, and it is wonderful to see it emerging from dereliction.

NEAREST MAJOR TOWN Verona
MAIN FEATURES beautifully maintained eighteenth-century garden in a fine rural setting
PRE-BOOKING yes
OWNER Contessa Loredan Rizzardi
ADDRESS loc. Pojega de Negrar, I-37011 Barolino
LOCATION Negrar is c. 18 kilometres north-west of Verona. Take the SS12 for Trento from Verona, turning off after c. 6 kilometres at Parona. Negrar is signposted off this road. On entering Negrar, turn right over the bridge, then immediately left, following the road for 1.5 kilometres to the villa. A sign indicates the car park for garden visitors. The custodian's house is in the yard by the car park
OPEN by appointment only; contact Amministrazione Guerrieri Rizzardi, tel.: +39 (0)45 7210028
ADMISSION free
WHEELCHAIRS no
REFRESHMENTS no, but the Rizzardi wines may be tasted here prior to purchase
LAVATORIES yes

The garden of Villa Rizzardi was laid out on the eve of the period in which *giardini all'italiana* were swept away, making space for those expanses of grass and woodland known as 'English' parks. The knowledge that it was the last garden of its kind to be created in Italy makes the perfectly maintained layout of Villa Rizzardi particularly precious.

The garden was designed for Count Antonio Rizzardi by Luigi Trezza and laid out between 1783 and 1791. However, the plans for the green theatre were not finalised till 1796.

The Rizzardi was a Veronese family whose wealth derived from foreign trade. Consequently, it was unusually well placed to comply with the fashion of the day by filling the garden with strange and wonderful plants imported from abroad. The property still belongs to the Rizzardi, though the villa was rebuilt in the nineteenth century.

The gardens lie on a slope above the villa. They are set out to create three distinct levels. On a first visit the simplicity of this layout is not immediately apparent. By screening the view between the different levels, and by distracting the visitor with glimpses of the hills beyond the garden, Trezza succeeded in concealing the basis of the design. It is only when you arrive at the cypress avenue that runs across the garden, intersecting each of its three levels, that you understand the design and the true proportions of the garden, which until that moment seem limitless.

One enters the garden at its highest level. A path flanked by ancient hornbeams leads to the *bosco*, which used to be planted with oak. During the Austrian occupation of the Veneto many of these were felled. However, the yew and beech that replaced them create a highly effective 'wild' area in the garden. The trees throw deep shadows, half concealing the humped forms of stone pumas that crouch on either side of the path. Perhaps the *bosco* should be seen as a substitute for the 'enclosure for wild beasts' that Pietro de Crescenzi advocated for the gardens of kings and noblemen in the fourteenth century. Miniature palms are all that remain of the mixture of indigenous and exotic plants that once carpeted the area, and no doubt reminded Count Rizzardi of the real jungles he had seen on his travels.

The *bosco* also conceals a 'Roman' ruin. The circular building was once surrounded by a box hedge, from which other hedges radiated like the points of a star. The boughs of the beech trees that meet high above it create the building's roof and fill it with soft, dappled light. The inside walls are decorated with stalactites collected from the Valpolicella. Niches between the doors contain statues, one of Diana, another of Hercules, each in violent combat with a wild beast.

On emerging from the *bosco* one arrives at the mid-point of the cypress avenue that climbs the slope, intersecting the walks that mark each level of the garden. At the top of the slope there is a charming belvedere embraced by two flights of steps. Putti stand on the octagonal balustrade that surrounds the terrace, overlooking a vista running the length of the avenue, only to be stopped by the cypresses grouped around a statue of Minerva at its far end. Trezza no doubt intended that the belvedere should give views over the surrounding countryside, unobscured by the trees that have now outgrown their intended height. The custodian's youngest daughter keeps house among the cypresses at the top of the avenue – she was seen disappearing among their leaves like the *genius loci*.

Trezza's green theatre, often described as the finest in Italy, lies to one side of the avenue. It is linked to the villa by a second avenue, which also marks the second level of the garden. The theatre was the last of the garden's features to be laid out, a fact that can be explained by Trezza's determination to find an ideal site for it. Audiences at the concerts held here each summer reap the rewards of his care – the acoustics are perfect. Trezza looked to the amphitheatres of ancient Greece for his inspiration. The auditorium consists of seven tiers of turf seats intersected by three flights of steps. Like the cypresses at the end of the avenue, the box hedges that separate the tiers have outgrown their purpose, making the seats unusable. However, 1000 people can be accommodated in the space below the stage. The beech hedge enclosing the theatre has been clipped to create niches for Pietro Muttoni's classical statues. Each is marked by a dome on the top of the hedge – a particularly delightful detail. The raised stage is more than 27 metres wide, with flats and a backdrop of clipped beech. The space between the stage and the high beech hedge that surrounds the theatre served as changing rooms. The stone benches in the wings were presumably provided for those overcome by stage fright.

The lowest level of the garden is marked by an alley of elm pleached to 6 metres. Rather than allowing them to meet and form a tunnel, the design dictates that they should be clipped to create a regular 120 centimetre gap between them. A *tapis vert* runs the length of the alley,

appearing to reflect the strip of sky above. In the spring, the beauty of this effect is heightened by the crocuses, snowdrops and violets that adorn the grass.

The villa lies at the far end of the alley overlooking a small parterre garden. Steps lead up from this level to the oval lemon garden above. The circular pool that once stood among the lemons has been converted to a swimming pool. However, the tritons and sea-creatures at its centre appear undisturbed by the change. The old *limonaie* that overlook the garden have been changed into covered terraces, used for alfresco tastings of the Rizzardi's famous wines. Standing between them one can enjoy a magnificent view of the hills framed by the avenue. The secret garden lies on the slope behind the villa and is not generally open to visitors. It is linked to the *piano nobile* by a bridge, currently a rather ugly metal affair. Terraces planted with green parterres ascend the slope, and a huge stalactite creates a cascade for the water which flows from the nymphaeum at the top.

The *giardino segreto* has rather lost its purpose now that it is overlooked by the new buildings on the other side of the road. It is the only place in the garden where neglect and the intrusion of the modern world combine to detract from the beauty of the original layout.

veneto

NEAREST MAJOR TOWN Verona

MAIN FEATURES two eighteenth-century gardens with magnificent views

PRE-BOOKING yes

OWNER Conte Giannino Marzotto

ADDRESS Piazza Trissino 2, I-36070 Trissino; tel.: +39 (0)445 962029, fax.: (0)445 962090

LOCATION Trissino is c. 50 kilometres north-east of Verona. Take the A4 for Padua, leaving it at the exit for Montecchio. Go through Montecchio Maggiore on the SS246 for Valdagno. Trissino is c. 11 kilometres from Montecchio, and the villa is signposted up the hill from the town centre

OPEN strictly by prior arrangement

ADMISSION free

WHEELCHAIRS no

REFRESHMENTS no

LAVATORIES no

There are two Trissino villas on the hillside overlooking the Agno Valley. The upper villa is built on the site of the castle that was the stronghold of the powerful Trissino family during the Middle Ages. The lower villa was built during the eighteenth century by the Trissino Riale, another branch of the same family.

More is known about the upper villa than the lower. During the fifteenth century the Trissino's feudal properties were absorbed into the Venetian Republic and their castle fell into disuse. In the fifteenth and sixteenth centuries alterations were made to the building, but it was not till 1722 that Francesco Muttoni replaced it with a new villa and garden around it. Muttoni received the Trissino commission in the wake of a visit to Rome where he had been deeply influenced by the work of Francesco Borromini. In Muttoni's original drawings for the villa and garden Borromini's style is certainly apparent. Had it been completed, the extraordinarily ambitious design would have turned the cliff on which the old castle was built into a series of terraces linked

by passages, walks, ramps tunnels and steps. In the 25 years before his death in 1748, Muttoni only managed to complete a fraction of the enormous task. When he died, Gerolamo dal Pozzo took his place. However, much of the original plan was abandoned.

Little is known of the history of the unfortunate lower villa. It was built at about the same time as the other villa. At the beginning of the nineteenth century it passed out of the hands of the Trissino Riale and became the property of the Trissino Baston, who still owned the upper villa. In 1841 it was destroyed by fire, rebuilt and then burnt again some years later and abandoned. The two villas passed out of the Trissino family to the Da Porto, and they now belong to the Marzotto.

Perched on its crag above the Agno Valley, the upper villa at Trissino can be seen from many miles away. The task of transforming the sheer and rocky hillside into a garden could scarcely have been more challenging and yet, if the difficulties of the site could be overcome, the magnificent setting ensured a startling result.

Muttoni's triple gateway acts as a flamboyant introduction to the garden. The ornate wrought-iron gates are crowned with an extraordinary mixture of scrolls, pinnacles, flaming torches and urns. The first gate was to lead to the terraces with which Muttoni planned to transform the hillside. It now creates a curious effect by opening out to thin air. The second gate leads to the lower terrace, and the third acts as an entrance to the triangular hanging garden.

The hanging garden is reached by a curiously complex route. A grotto containing a water-worn statue of Pan conceals the base of a curving ramp. The ramp leads up through a tunnel, and emerges on a balustraded terrace overlooking the magnificent view. Rough grass and weeds now swamp the hanging garden, which was intended to be laid down to lawn. A minaret built on the retaining wall encloses a spiral staircase. Sadly, it is too decrepit to be safe, but Muttoni's intention was that it should be used as an alternative route to the lower terrace.

Dal Pozzo is said to have had the ingenious idea of linking the hanging garden to the villa by means of a long balcony. The balcony runs around the *piano nobile*, along the wall that encloses the secret garden, and emerges on the belvedere.

veneto

The lower terrace is lined with pots of lemon and classical statues. It runs below the retaining wall of the hanging garden and at its far end opens out into a curious hexagonal garden. The trees on the slope below have grown to such a height that they now enclose the garden on two sides. This detracts from Muttoni's intention, which must surely have been to create a garden that seemed to hang in space above the breathtaking view. Scrolled stone seats are set into the angles of the hexagonal wall. The garden is laid out with a formal pattern of geometric beds divided by gravel paths. The beds are surrounded by raised stone borders forming elaborate patterns that incorporate the Trissino family crest. These borders must be unique and it would be tragic if they were lost to the neglect that threatens to destroy them.

During the nineteenth century the Trissino turned the wooded area immediately behind the terrace into a memorial garden. Family monuments and tombstones stand among the trees, creating a fascinating and rather lugubrious effect.

One of the many paths that lead through the woods runs below the huge supporting structure of the hanging garden. The other retaining wall forms the boundary of the secret garden outside the villa. It is covered in roses and decorated with niches containing statues. Opposite the main entrance of the villa's new wing is a sizeable grotto. Currently it enshrines the wreck of a sports car, a weirdly disturbing sight that commemorates a lucky escape by Count Marzotto, once a well-known racing driver. A curving drive runs down through the woods from the end of the lower terrace to the villa below. The gardens of the two villas bear no relationship to each other, and the name of the lower garden's designer is unknown. At the beginning of the nineteenth century there was a plan to terrace the hillside, thus creating a link between the villas. However, the death of the architect, Ottone Calderai, halted the plans.

The lower villa still stands, but it has no roof and the ground floor has been used to house animals. The bricked-up windows of the main façade once overlooked the wide terrace below. The balustrade is overgrown with Russian vine, and the grass covering the steps to the lower garden is so long that a path has to be beaten through it.

Below the terrace is a vast lawn with a large hexagonal pool at its centre. The effect of this simple layout is enormously spacious. It is overlooked on all sides by an infinite number of statues attributed to Orazio Marinali and Giacomo Cassetti. They stand in a circle around the pool, line the balustrades that form the boundary of the garden and even look down from the upper terrace. The effect is of a vast and courtly ball where the guests are an incongruous mixture of Venetians and ancient Romans. Most of the figures were produced in 1715, and the weather has been doing its worst since then. Many have lost limbs, and all are covered in lichen and vine. It is almost impossible to read their names, which were once inscribed at the base of each pedestal.

On the far side of the pool the garden's rectangular form is broken by a semicircular terrace. Flights of steps lead down to what was once a lower walk, and is now a wilderness of nettles. Neptune looks out from the brambles beneath the retaining wall.

Much of the lower garden has been restored since our first visit, and the meadow below the terrace has been brought back to a lawn.

tuscany (toscana)

Tuscany runs from the central mountain ranges of Italy west to the coast. It contains a wide variety of landscape, from the Maremma marshes to the Apennine heights. The best-known region is undoubtedly the Chianti. The summers are hot, and the winters cold but short.

As the Papacy has been to the history of Rome, so were the Medici to Tuscany. During the fifteenth century Cosimo de'Medici and his grandson Lorenzo (il Magnifico) made the city the birthplace of the Renaissance. The Medici were subsequently expelled from Florence on several occasions, but always managed to return. In 1569, the Grand Duchy of Tuscany was created, with another Cosimo de'Medici as the first Grand Duke.

The Medici line became increasingly decadent and died out in 1743, when Tuscany passed to the House of Lorraine. From 1865 to 1871 Florence was the capital of Italy.

With a few exceptions, the typical early Tuscan garden tends towards the domestic in scale. A cypress avenue, a bowling alley, a few garden rooms with simple parterres; visual magnificence may be provided by a grand view, according to Leon Battista Alberti's recommendations. The architectural grandeur of the Roman style was resisted in Tuscany throughout the Renaissance.

NEAREST MAJOR TOWN Florence

MAIN FEATURES sixteenth-century ducal garden of the Medici, cypress avenue, island, excellent statuary

PRE-BOOKING no

OWNER the State

ADDRESS Piazza Pitti 1, I-50125 Florence

LOCATION behind the Palazzo Pitti in central Florence; entered via the ticket office inside the main entrance to the palace

OPEN November to February, 9.00–16.30; March and April, 9.00–17.30; May to August, 9.00–19.30; September and October, 9.00–17.30; closed first and last Monday of each month

ADMISSION L4000

WHEELCHAIRS yes

REFRESHMENTS yes

LAVATORIES yes

Palazzo Pitti, begun in 1453 to the design of Filippo Brunelleschi, is named after its original owner, Luca Pitti. Luca was one of the wealthiest men in Florence, and was used as a political pawn by the Medici throughout his life: they gave him 20,000 florins towards building costs in return for political services rendered. Ironically, in 1549 Eleanora, wife of Cosimo 1 de'Medici, bought the unfinished palace from Luca's descendants for a mere 9000 florins. There are no records of any significant gardens before Eleanora's purchase.

Eleanora, who was considered an '*insupportabile gravità*', or an intolerable bore, by the Florentines, also purchased the hillside behind the palace. The greater part of the land was owned by the Borgoli family, hence the name Boboli. The last Borgoli to farm the land apparently never recovered from parting with it. His is one of the very few attested ghosts in Italy – and is said to be seen about the gardens to this day.

In 1549 Niccolò Tribolo was commissioned to design gardens for

tuscany (toscana)

the new palace while continuing his work on another of Cosimo's gardens at Castello (page 193). The rough, hillside site was levelled, manured and planted with ilex, fir and cypress.

Tribolo's design celebrated Cosimo I's achievement in bringing fresh water to Florence. A 9-metre circle of granite, quarried on the island of Elba and transported up the Arno River to Florence, was used as the basin for a colossal statue of Oceanus, the source of all seas and rivers, executed by Giambologna (the original is in the Bargello). The statue was completed in 1576 and placed behind the palazzo, on the site of the amphitheatre. It was moved to the Isolotto in 1637 when the amphitheatre was built.

Tribolo died in 1550, allegedly worn out by the massive scale of the project. The task of constructing the garden was taken up by Bernado Buontalenti, Bartolommeo Ammanati and later the Parigi brothers.

In 1560, Cosimo, Eleanora and their children moved to the Palazzo Pitti from their cramped quarters in Palazzo Vecchio. Work on the building had not finished, but it is said that Eleanora could wait no longer to move into the more spacious surroundings. There was no garden at the Palazzo Vecchio and her collection of rare plants and animals had been kept on a balcony. Sadly Eleanora died within a couple of years of moving.

Unlike those at Castello, the gardens at Boboli have no unifying iconographic theme. The fountains all celebrate Cosimo's viaducts and the fresh water they carried, but their grandeur was more important than their message. The gardens were rarely used as a place of individual refreshment or retreat. They have always been 'public' gardens in the sense that their principal function was the display of Medici wealth and power. It was to this end that a series of festivities was held

tuscany (toscana)

during the sixteenth and seventeenth centuries. One of the most famous was the Naumachia of 1589, performed as part of the elaborate marriage celebrations for Ferdinando I and Christine of Lorraine. The sunken courtyard behind the palace was flooded, and 18 Christian galleons were seen to besiege a Turkish castle. In 1631 the hollow behind the palace, whose potential Tribolo had largely ignored, was transformed into an amphitheatre with six tiers of stone seats which provided an ideal setting for festivities on an even grander scale. The marriage of the future Cosimo III to Marguerite Louise d'Orleans was marked by a performance of *Il Mondo Festeggiante*, a combination of masque, pageant and equestrian ballet in which Cosimo appeared as Hercules in jewel-studded armour. There were 20,000 spectators, but unfortunately the performance failed to impress the princess. Asked if she liked Florence, she replied that she would like it better if it were nearer Paris.

With the unification of Italy the gardens passed to the State, and they have been open to the public ever since.

On entering the garden from the palace, you will find yourself in a sunken courtyard containing Ammanati's Grotto of Moses, a large pool inside which, delightfully, putti are swimming.

The amphitheatre above the courtyard was designed by Giulio Parigi and built in 1637. It is a simple semicircle with six tiers of stone benches. However, the severe and ponderous design was created while elsewhere in the country the Baroque was in full swing. It is extraordinary how little the Tuscan designers learned from their Roman counterparts – despite the existence of four Medici popes.

From the amphitheatre a double flight of steps leads up to Tribolo's pool and the Fountain of Neptune (1565) by Stoldo Lorenzi, which

once stood above the Grotto of Moses. Higher still stands Giambologna's great statue of Abundance, erected to symbolise the benevolent rule of Ferdinando II de'Medici. It was originally made as a portrait of Joanna of Austria, wife of Francesco I, but her husband lost interest in both his wife and her statue. Below the walls of Fort Belvedere to the north is the Kaffeehaus of 1776, where there is a small restaurant with a fine view of the city.

Walking in the other direction you reach the splendid cypress avenue, which descends steeply through a labyrinth of paths, groves

tuscany (toscana)

and pergolas. It is lined with classical statues and was originally grassed over. The effect of the shaded, mossy descent, broken at intervals by shallow stone steps, must have been beautiful. A few steps remain, but sadly the path was gravelled over at the turn of the last century. The groves on each side are what remain of the *ragnaie*. The maze and botanical gardens were in this area; these have not survived.

At the foot of the avenue is a large oval pool and lemon island, the 'Isolotto'. This delightful Baroque fantasy is probably the most attractive feature of the gardens and was laid out by Alfonso Parigi in 1618. The island is so named because it is linked to the shore by bridges lined with lemon trees. The gates at the end of each bridge are crowned with goats, in reference to Cosimo III's astrological symbol. Giambologna's *Oceanus* stands in the centre of the island supported by personifications of the three greatest rivers known at that time: the Nile, the Ganges and the Euphrates. There is also a dramatic Perseus riding through the water to the rescue of Andromeda, who is chained to her rock at the far end of the pool.

The line of the cypress avenue continues directly towards the Porta Romana exit. Alternatively you can turn right towards the huge *limonaia*, which takes you back to the amphitheatre.

On leaving the garden by the Palazzo Pitti exit you pass Buontalenti's magnificent grotto, built in 1583. It is the largest and most important grotto of the period and it has been beautifully restored. Its three chambers are richly decorated with shell and mosaic. Inside are Giambologna's *Venus* and a copy of one of Michelangelo's *Slaves*, the original of which is in the Accademia delle Belle Arti in Florence.

NEAREST MAJOR TOWN Florence
MAIN FEATURES fine botanical garden
with sixteenth-century origins
PRE-BOOKING no
OWNER University of Florence
ADDRESS Via P A Micheli 3, I-50121
Florence
LOCATION entrance through garden

offices on Via P A Micheli
OPEN May to September: Monday,
Wednesday, Friday, 9.00–12.00
ADMISSION free
WHEELCHAIRS yes, having negotiated
steps at entrance
REFRESHMENTS yes
LAVATORIES yes

The Giardino dei Semplici is one of the oldest botanical gardens in the world. It was founded by Cosimo I de'Medici in 1545, only a couple of years after he had founded the botanical garden attached to the university at Pisa.

The garden's original purpose was the cultivation of *semplici*, medicinal plants or simples. Cosimo commissioned Niccolò Tribolo to design the new garden. Tribolo was already engaged in the vast project of creating a garden for the Medici villa at Castello (page 193). Only four years later, with both Castello and the Giardino dei Semplici still in progress, Cosimo presented him with the mammoth task of designing the Giardino di Boboli (page 147). The following year he died, perhaps exhausted by the extent of his responsibilities.

The site chosen for the Giardino dei Semplici was square and surrounded by high walls. Records of the original layout and planting by Leopoldo del Migliore have survived, though in book form and published more than a century later in 1648. It was not until the end of the eighteenth century that Tribolo's original design was altered. An engraving made in 1748 by Pier Antonio Micheli, then the garden's director, shows a series of regular beds divided by paths and trees. At the centre of the garden Tribolo created an octagonal space shaded by trees and decked with terracotta pots of flowering plants. He commissioned Antonio Lorenzi, a pupil, to make a fountain to stand there. According to the sixteenth-century biographer Giorgio Vasari, beautiful aquatic animals carved from marble swam in the water. Tribolo also commissioned numerous sculptures to stand in the garden, though the only one to survive is a bust of Aesculapius attributed to Antonio Gino Lorenzi di Settignano.

Luca Ghini was responsible for the planting of the garden. He was a professional botanist from Bologna who held the Chair of Botany at Pisa and who had already collaborated with Cosimo in the foundation of the botanic garden there two years earlier. Under Ghini the garden was soon stocked with a fine collection of plants, many of which were contributed by Cosimo's friends or by botanists working in other parts of the country. Cosimo may well have added specimens to the collection. His interest in rare and exotic plants extended beyond the foundation of public institutions. His and Eleanora's collection, housed largely at Castello, consisted of plants brought to him from all over the world. Many specimens were obtained from the far-flung colonies of the Venetian Republic; while Jesuit missionaries returning from the Far East were eagerly awaited by Cosimo and many other avid collectors.

Ghini died in 1556 and Cosimo survived him by nearly 20 years, but after the demise of both men the garden sank into obscurity. In 1718, under Cosimo III de'Medici, the garden came under the administration of the Florentine Botanical Society, and Micheli, the founder of the society, became the garden's director. Under his guidance the botanical collection was greatly enriched and the garden became world famous.

Another high point in the garden's history occurred towards the end

of the nineteenth century when Teodoro Caruel became director. Under his care the garden was developed and the conservatories, which are still used today, were erected. Today the garden is attached to the University of Florence and it continues to be a valuable centre for botanical and agricultural research.

The garden is divided into regular beds flanked by paths and an enormous variety of different trees, many of which are several centuries old. The oldest is a common yew planted by Micheli in 1720. More than 5000 specimens of woody and herbaceous plants from all over the world are displayed in outdoor beds and hothouses. For anyone interested in herbal medicine the collection of *semplici* will be a particular attraction. Each plant is marked with its family, genus, species and the part used for its active ingredients.

In the hot houses are numerous tropical plants. The smaller greenhouses are devoted to individual species. For example, one houses a collection of ferns, another serves as the orchid house and a third is devoted to the begonia. The nature of the garden makes a specialist guide almost essential. The University of Florence has produced a detailed and readable botanical guide which may be purchased – in translation – from the office at the main entrance.

NEAREST MAJOR TOWN Florence
MAIN FEATURES traditional Tuscan garden, secret garden, box parterre, views over city
PRE-BOOKING yes
OWNER Benedetti family
ADDRESS Via Pian dei Giullari 3, Arcetri, Florence
LOCATION leaving Florence by the Porta Romana, take Via del Poggio Imperiale. At Poggio Imperiale, turn left into Via di San Leonardo. Turn right into Via del Pian dei Giullari. Villa Capponi is on the left
OPEN strictly by written arrangement with Signora Maria Teresa Benedetti
ADMISSION at the discretion of the family
WHEELCHAIRS yes
REFRESHMENTS no
LAVATORIES yes

Ginodi Lodovico Capponi is known to have bought this hillside villa in February 1572. As a member of the illustrious Capponi family, he held a privileged position in the political and social world of the Florentine Republic. Almost immediately, Capponi set about transforming the rough herb and vegetable patch below the house into a sophisticated garden, and it is thought that the walled garden below the terrace and the lemon garden can be attributed to this period in the history of the property.

The villa belonged to the Capponi family for more than 300 years. In 1882 it was bought by Lady Scott, a daughter of the Duke of Portland and grandmother to the present Queen Mother. It was during this time that the garden became famous: Gertrude Jekyll, Jeffrey Jellicoe and Queen Victoria are numbered among its visitors. After Lady Scott's death the villa again became the home of expatriates. The Price family from England lived there for some time and then sold the property to the Cliffords of Pennsylvania. When the present owners

bought it, they were the first Italians to live there for almost a century.

It is extraordinarily fortunate that each of the villa's owners was so devoted to its garden: not only has it been preserved by each generation, but also it has expanded and developed.

The house is situated on a southern hillside overlooking the Arno valley. Like the garden of La Gamberaia (page 175), which was also designed for the Capponi, it catches the breeze on the most stifling of days and commands a glorious view of the city. The villa presents an austere face to the road from Poggio Imperiale, but on the garden side its pretty façade is swathed in wisteria and decorated by a small loggia. Wedges of clipped box stand between the downstairs windows.

The garden, which was built largely during the seventeenth century, falls into three distinct areas. There is a magnificent grass bowling alley beneath the walls of the villa, which may well have been designed in response to Leon Battista Alberti's belief that every garden should have an area set aside for outdoor games. Opposite the door to the house, a pair of wrought-iron gates frames the distant hills, olive groves and cypresses. The swags of Banksian rose swathing the pillars to either side complete the beauty of the view.

At its north-western end, the bowling alley gives way to a wide terrace overlooking the spectacular view. Pots of hibiscus, pelargonium and jasmine add colour to this area, which is also decorated by a fine loggia built for Lady Scott. It was her inspired idea to use *pietra serena* columns, salvaged when the market place in Florence was demolished to make way for Piazza della Repubblica.

At its other extreme, the bowling alley leads into the second original sixteenth-century element of the garden. Pillars topped by terracotta griffins flank the entrance to the lemon garden. The area is laid out with well-clipped square and diamond parterres divided by neat, gravel paths. The lemons in their pots stand at the centre of each parterre. In spring, the pots are surrounded by a blue mist of forget-me-not. More lemons are arranged around a fish pool at the centre of the garden. The area is enclosed by a high Baroque wall, decorated with curves and pedestals, and surmounted by terracotta urns.

Below the terrace, the ground falls away to the *giardino segreto*, the

third original element of the garden. Until this century the garden could only be entered from the house: an underground passage led from the cellars and emerged behind the grotto in the retaining wall of the terrace. The grotto, decorated with tufa and stalactites, remains, but another entrance has been made. The complete enclosure of the garden creates a perfect sun trap and the air is scented by Banksian roses, wisteria and jasmine that thrive against its walls. The wall is similar in design to that of the lemon garden and is known to have been built for Capponi. Windows have been made to give glimpses of the beautiful hillside below.

Steps lead down to a lower garden, enclosed by enormous domes of clipped yew, added by Lady Scott at the end of the nineteenth century. Parterres, gravel paths and topiary surround the rectangular pool at the centre of the garden.

A gate from this second garden room leads into the area chosen by the Cliffords for their swimming pool. The architect Cecil Pinsent was commissioned to create the oblong 'Roman bath', decorated by spouting dolphins at one end. The area is made completely private by a huge cypress hedge, while niches in the hedge hold stone benches and statues. Sadly, the pool is no longer used.

An informal grassy walk, lined by iris and anemone each spring, leads out of the garden, through the olive grove and orchard, returning finally to the main garden beyond the villa.

NEAREST MAJOR TOWN Siena
MAIN FEATURES seventeenth-century garden in a fine hillside setting, the baid
PRE-BOOKING yes
OWNER Lord Lambton
ADDRESS Cetinale, Sovicille, I-53098 Siena; tel. +39 (0)577 311147
LOCATION Cetinale is c. 12 kilometres west of Siena. From Siena take the SS73 (Massa Marittima) and after c. 7 kilometres turn right for Sovicille.

Two kilometres further turn right for Ancaiano (unsurfaced road). On rejoining the main road turn right and follow signs to Cetinale
OPEN by appointment only by letter or telephone
ADMISSION free
WHEELCHAIRS yes
REFRESHMENTS no
LAVATORIES yes

It would be difficult to do better than to quote the words of Joseph Forsyth, an antiquarian and traveller who visited Villa Chigi, as it then was, in around 1800. 'Cetinale', he wrote, 'which lies in a wide scraggy oak-wood about ten miles from Siena, owes its rise and celebrity to the remorse of an amorous cardinal who, to appease the ghost of a murdered rival, transformed a gloomy plantation of cypress into a penitential Thebais, and acted there all the austerities of an Egyptian hermit'.

The 'amorous cardinal' was Flavio Chigi, Prince of Farnese, Duke of Ariccia and Prince of the Holy Roman Empire. The Chigi were rich Sienese bankers with clients ranging from popes to English kings. Chigi was nephew to Pope Alexander II and, it is said, the last cardinal to be appointed solely by virtue of a family relationship. He employed the Roman architect Carlo Fontana, a pupil of Gianlorenzo Bernini, to add to the original villa and to design its gardens in 1680.

Chigi must have been an unusual man. Harold Acton translates a

Latin inscription on the villa as: 'Whoever you are who approach, that which may seem horrible to you is pleasing to myself. If it appeals to you, remain. If it bores you, go away! Each is equally agreeable to me'. You wonder if Cosimo III de'Medici noticed this inscription when he was entertained at Cetinale by Cardinal Chigi in 1691.

After the cardinal's death the villa passed to his nephews, the Chigi-Zondadari. It remained in their possession until acquired by the present owner in 1977. The villa had been uninhabited since 1959 and the garden was completely overgrown.

Cetinale is enclosed by a great arm of mountainside densely covered with oak woods. As at Il Bozzolo (page 62), only a garden plan of the utmost simplicity could hold its own in so grand a setting. Fontana's plan could hardly have been simpler. Everything stands on a single axis which runs for about 5 kilometres straight from the valley, through the ground floor of the villa to the mountain skyline.

The foot of the axis is marked by a great statue of Hercules standing among the woods. The line dips down to a stream, and then up towards the villa as a *tapis vert* between double rows of ilex. Passing through the gate and receiving a noisy welcome from the household dogs, you enter the nineteenth-century walled lemon garden in front of the villa. On the left are the *limonaia* and the family chapel, both designed by Fontana. Statues of Summer and Spring by Giuseppe Mazzuoli decorate the central path.

Fontana also added two wings to the south front of the villa and created an open loggia (later closed in). A shaded lime walk runs around the building to the main entrance on the west side. Here Fontana added a double marble staircase which runs up to the *piano nobile* on the first floor. This is not a typical feature in Tuscany. Fontana was following traditional Roman custom by reserving the ground floor for the kitchen, store rooms and other functional areas. Both façades were decorated with Baroque motifs of the Papal Mitre, the Keys of the Kingdom of Heaven, Chigi coats of arms and marquis' coronets. A string-course was added between the floors.

A broad grass avenue runs towards the ilex-covered hillside and it draws the eye to the focal point of the design, the hermitage – or *romitorio* – placed far above on the skyline.

Beneath the retaining wall to the left of the *viale* is the garden originally laid out at the turn of the century by the English wife of one of the Chigi. This area has been beautifully planted by Claire Ward who has created a wonderfully romantic garden heady with the scent of honeysuckle and old English roses. Pergolas divide the densely planted beds of cottage garden plants and vegetables, all thriving on a diet of Tuscan sunshine and copious watering.

The end of the cypress avenue is marked by a brick gateway ornamented with busts and fifteenth-century statues. From this point an open grass walk continues to the green theatre, beyond which is a gate leading to the woods beyond. This is the beginning of the *scala santa*, a staircase of about 200 rough stone steps leading up through the woods to the *romitorio*.

A ramp leads out of the theatre to the right and into the holy wood or 'Thebaid' referred to by Forsyth. A fairly common theme during the seventeenth century, the name derives from the communities of the Desert Fathers around Thebes in Egypt in the first centuries AD. Paintings on the subject were often used to decorate rooms reserved for meditation and prayer. At Cetinale the Thebaid consists of a number of grassy forest walks lined with frescoed chapels, statues of the disciples and personifications of penitence. The Palio – the horse race run in the centre of Siena – took place in the Thebaid several times between 1690 and 1710. Mazzuoli carved the symbols of the winning contrade out of stone and many carvings still line the main walk through the wood.

It is worth making the climb to the hermitage, for the view is glorious. The building itself is much larger than it seems from the villa and it was inhabited by monks until the end of the last century. Five storeys high, it has a central alcove containing a great cross of Lorraine, which is as tall as the building itself. Niches at each extremity of the cross hold busts of Christ and the Evangelists. The interior sadly has been vandalised but it is still possible to climb to the top and see Cetinale laid out below you, with white doves circling over its roof and the olive groves spreading around it.

NEAREST MAJOR TOWN Florence
MAIN FEATURES eighteenth-century garden on a level site outside Florence, twentieth-century green theatre and maze
PRE-BOOKING only groups
OWNER Conti Guicciardini-Corsi-Salviati
ADDRESS Via Gramsci 462, Sesto Fiorentino, Florence

LOCATION Sesto Fiorentino is c. 9 kilometres north-west of Florence. Via Gramsci is the main road into Sesto from Florence, and the villa is on the left just before the town
OPEN May to October, Tuesday and Friday, 15.00–dusk
ADMISSION free
WHEELCHAIRS yes
REFRESHMENTS no
LAVATORIES yes

Villa Corsi Salviati has belonged to the family since the sixteenth century. Unlike the majority of its Tuscan counterparts, the garden occupies a level site. This may in part explain the extraordinary facility with which successive generations have changed it to conform with the fashions of the day.

When Simone di Jacopo Corsi bought the villa in 1502 it was a simple farmhouse: the garden behind it consisted of a few patches of lawn arranged around a fountain. It was not until the beginning of the seventeenth century that three additional areas were added to the layout. The lawns were turned into grass parterres and bounded to the east by a *bosco*. Beyond the trees was a kitchen garden, enclosed on three sides by walls and on the fourth by a *limonaia*. A bowling green stretched along the east wing of the villa. To the west, the parterres were bounded by a walled lemon garden arranged around a circular pool with the rabbit island. A *ragnaia* was created beyond the southern boundary of the parterre garden. The villa itself was extended by the addition of a loggia and a large aviary was built against the west wall. In 1738 the villa was altered once again by Marchese Antonio Corsi, who responded to the fashion of the day by adding a graceful Baroque façade. The two balustraded belvederes on either side of the central block also date from this period. The aviary was transformed into an open loggia.

An engraving executed by Giuseppe Zocchi in 1740 records the results of the Marquis' work on the garden. The wall that divided the parterres from the lemon garden was taken down. The rabbit island was removed and the circular pool was incorporated in the central layout. Zocchi's print also shows several jets of water rising from the surface of the pool, in imitation of the French fountains that had become so fashionable. Wrought-iron fences and ornate gates decorated with statues surrounded the garden just as they do today. The *ragnaia,* which like the lemon garden and rabbit island was too practical for the Marquis' taste, was replaced by a short canal divided by little cascades. The *bosco* was extended into the area that had served as a kitchen garden.

During the nineteenth century the garden was altered yet again. The *bosco* was transformed into a romantic wood with two mounds, a ruined 'castle' and a small lake with an island and rustic hut. Palm trees were planted behind the villa and two greenhouses were built to shelter Marquis Amerigo Corsi's rare and exotic plants, for which the garden soon became famous.

In 1907 Marchese Giulio Guicciardini Corsi Salviati – the father of the present owner – set about restoring the eighteenth-century layout. Although the romantic woods were left largely intact, he pulled down the greenhouses and reinstated the parterres with a faithful recon-

struction of the eighteenth-century layout. Looking at the parterre garden today it is hard to believe that it dates only from the beginning of the twentieth century.

The garden is enclosed on one side by the delightful façade of the villa. The woods lie to the west, and to the south and east it is bounded by an ornate wall and a fence which is divided by pillars and adorned with numerous statues. Many are missing, but that remain include animals, classical figures, Tuscan peasants, urns and torches.

A simple fountain stands at the centre of the garden and around it statues and stone benches are arranged in a circle. The parterre beds, planted with brightly coloured annuals, form a series of small diamonds and rectangles, an arrangement popular in the eighteenth century. Pots of lemons among the parterres add to the colourful layout.

The oblong pool west of the parterres also existed in the eighteenth century. Water flows into it from grotesque masks that decorate the walls and statues of the Four Seasons mark each corner of the pool, which is enclosed by a balustrade decorated with terracotta pots of trailing geranium. A loggia at the far end, which replaced the seventeenth-century aviary, is frescoed with classical ruins. A circular lily pond lies beyond the pool. It originally surrounded the rabbit island and features in the foreground of Zocchi's print.

The eighteenth-century canal can still be seen cutting through the old *ragnaia* that lay opposite the villa, beyond the boundary of the parterre garden. It is made of 13 separate basins divided by little cascades once decorated with water jets. The apparent length of the canal was increased by a fountain at its far end decorated with a *trompel'oeil* created from *spugne* and mosaics. The ilex wood to the east of the parterres was planted to create shady paths and groves. Very little is left of the statues that once stood among the trees. The romantic lake, spanned by a decorative bridge, is somewhat overgrown, and so is the maze that the Marquis planted on the site of the old greenhouses. Having no record of the seventeenth-century design he drew his plans from the maze at the royal palace of Hampton Court near London.

A green theatre lies below the east wing of the villa and in front of the *limonaia*. Although not a feature of the original layout, it was built during the restoration of the garden. One of the nineteenth-century mounds was used as a foundation and its design was drawn from the plans of the theatre at Castle Mirabell in Salzburg, Austria. The narrow, mossy stage is enclosed by wings of clipped box. Apollo stands at the back of the stage on a pillar supported by turtles. The prompter's box is made from clipped box and enclosed by a dome of ivy.

NEAREST MAJOR TOWN Siena
MAIN FEATURES small, seventeenth-century garden overlooking Siena, ilex tunnels, green theatre, *ragnaia*
PRE-BOOKING yes
OWNER Avv. Giovanni Ginaneschi
ADDRESS Via Ventena 8, I-53100 Siena
LOCATION from Siena follow signs for the station. Turn right over the railway line, following signs for the d'Osservanza. Take the Via dell'Osservanza. Continue for c. 500 metres, turning left on to Via del Paradiso. The road forks and Via Ventena is the left fork. The villa is to the right of the road and the entrance is at the far end
OPEN strictly by appointment by letter or telephone
ADMISSION free
WHEELCHAIRS yes, with assistance
REFRESHMENTS no
LAVATORIES no

These gardens are known to have been laid out in 1620, when the villa was built for the de'Gori. It remained in family possession until shortly before the Second World War when it was bought by the Muratori. Signora Ginaneschi (née Muratori) still lives there today. During the war the villa suffered bomb damage and although everything else was destroyed, the garden and the villa's beautiful Baroque façade miraculously escaped. The villa's historical importance was such that it was rebuilt behind the façade, in accordance with the original plans.

The seventeenth-century terraces that once lay in front of the villa disappeared long ago. However, four of the garden's original features have survived and combine to create an interesting and unusual layout.

The villa stands at the junction of two long tunnels of gnarled ilex. One tunnel leads to the green theatre. It used to double as the entrance avenue. Over the centuries the roof of the tunnel grew lower and lower, until it became imperative to create the new gateway used today.

The green theatre is enclosed by a double ilex hedge, which allows the actors to move about back-stage without being spotted by the audience. The wings are formed by a series of smaller cypress hedges, and a curved flight of shallow steps serves as seats for the audience. Turf and pebbles were used to form an elaborate pattern of beds between the seats and the stage. The turf has gone, but the slates that used to edge the beds remain and form a distinctive pattern. Although it is rather overgrown, the theatre would be a memorable setting for a performance of almost any kind. It was used most recently by the Ginaneschi children for their own productions.

The second tunnel leads away from the villa at right angles to the first. Olive and fruit trees grow on either side of it, in what may once have been the terraced garden. The *ragnaia* is at the far end of the tunnel and consists of ilex planted in a series of concentric circles, and intersected by four slightly sunken stone paths. The *ragnaia* was concealed in a central clearing and was made of netting smeared with bird lime. As if this was not bad enough, the decoy birds used to attract victims had to be blinded. This was said to make them sing, a singing decoy apparently being more effective than a silent one. Sadly, bird snares were a common feature in Italian gardens, providing both sport and sustenance. The one at de'Gori is a particularly precious example, as very few have survived the passage of time.

In front of the villa clipped cypresses form curious arches, and screen a glorious view of Siena. It is on account of these arches and its hillside position that the villa can so easily be seen from the city.

tuscany (toscana)

NEAREST MAJOR TOWN Florence

MAIN FEATURES perfect Tuscan garden, water parterre, sunken garden, lovely rural setting

PRE-BOOKING only groups; pre-book for Sundays

OWNER Signor and Signora Marchi Zalum

ADDRESS Via Rossellino 72, I-50135 Florence; tel.: +39 (0)55 697205

LOCATION Settignano is beyond Fiesole to the north-east of Florence. Via Rossellino is beyond the main village piazza on the right. The villa is on the right after c. 2 kilometres. Parking is available outside the main gates. Note that coaches cannot proceed beyond the piazza

OPEN Monday to Friday, 9.00–12.00, 14.00–18.00

ADMISSION L12,000

WHEELCHAIRS yes

REFRESHMENTS no

LAVATORIES no

Villa Gamberaia is named after the first of a succession of owners. Matteo Gamberelli, for whom it was built at the beginning of the sixteenth century, was a stone mason. His sons, Bernardo and Giovanni, worked as architects under the name of Rossellino. Bernardo designed the Piccolomini Palace at Pienza for Pius II.

At the beginning of the seventeenth century the property passed to Zenobi Lappi. In 1900 a broken shield was found in the garden bearing the inscription 'zenobus lapit fundavit MDCX'. This probably means that Lapi virtually rebuilt the existing structure. When he died in 1619 the property was inherited by his nephews, Jacopo and Andrea. Andrea is said to have developed a passion for building fountains and he secured a good supply of water to the garden by purchasing various nearby springs, and then bought the right to pipe the water over adjacent land. In fact, in 1636 he was brought to court by a neighbour after he diverted the water supply to her villa. Sadly, there is no

record of the garden Andrea created and it is hardly surprising that on his death in 1688 the villa had to be mortgaged to pay off the debts.

In 1717 Gamberaia passed to the Capponi, and under their care the garden assumed its present form. The architect is unknown and Giuseppe Zocchi's engraving, which was made between 1735 and 1750, is the earliest record of the garden.

At the end of the nineteenth century Princess Ghyka of Serbia bought the villa and lived there with her American companion, Miss Blood. It is to the princess that we owe the creation of the water parterre. According to Iris Origo, the author who grew up at Villa Medici in Fiesole (page 203), the princess was once a great beauty. As she grew older she took to wearing a veil, and only left the villa to swim in the parterre pools at dawn, and to walk in the avenue after dark.

During the Second World War Gamberaia was virtually destroyed by bombing raids. Signor Marcello Marchi discovered it after the war and decided to restore the house and gardens to their original form. The garden has long been famous and he referred to numerous old prints, maps and photographs for guidance. Sadly, Signor Marchi died in 1989 and the property was left to his four children. Both the house and the gardens are being beautifully restored at the time of writing.

For generations Gamberaia has been cited as one of the most perfect examples of garden architecture. In an area of barely 1.25 hectares it combines, in Edith Wharton's words, 'almost every typical excellence of the old Italian garden: free circulation of air about the house; abundance of water; variety of effect produced by the skilful use of different levels and, finally, breadth and simplicity of composition'.

The gates swing open on to an imposing cypress avenue that serves to frame a small portion of the villa. It is a simple, rectangular building. The long east wall is extended at either end by curious flying arcades. To the north, the arcade links the villa to the chapel, thus completing a continuous line of buildings that runs down to the gatehouse. To the south, a spiral staircase is concealed inside the arcade, linking the piano nobile to the parterre garden below.

The villa stands at the mid-point of the bowling green, which is one of Gamberaia's most beautiful features. The smooth lawn stretches the length of the garden, spanning c. 180 metres. On one side it is flanked almost continuously by buildings, and on the other it is enclosed by the high retaining wall of the upper terraces. The wall is surmounted by urns and is decorated with painted panels. In effect, the bowling alley resembles a quiet street, paved with grass and peopled by statues. At its northern end the perspective is closed by a nymphaeum in the shade of a group of ancient cypresses. Water flowing into the structure trickles over a mossy tussock. The walls are decorated with *spugne*, mosaics and bas-reliefs, and the fountain inside is guarded by a dryad holding a trident and by two lions. At the other end of the alley a statue of Diana is silhouetted against a magnificent view of the Arno valley. The garden seems to extend beyond its boundaries into the olive groves and vineyards that surround it.

Opposite the villa the retaining wall is interrupted by a pair of wrought-iron gates decorated with the Florentine lily. They open into a sunken garden enclosed on three sides by the retaining wall of the upper terraces. Bands of *spugne* and 'rustic' stonework divide the wall into panels and smiling statues stand in niches set into it. Four flights of balustraded steps link the garden to the lemon garden on one side and an area of *bosco* on the other. The shady *bosco* on the other side of the sunken garden is planted with ilex and cypress. This 'wild' area, an essential element in the Renaissance garden, creates a pleasing contrast with the manicured perfection of the bowling alley.

The lemon garden is set out in front of the *limonaia* and lies on a level with the *piano nobile* of the villa. Beyond it a path winds down through the trees to the end of the bowling alley.

A loggia on the *piano nobile* of the villa's south façade overlooks the water parterre. This area of the garden has always been a parterre, and it is still laid out in the traditional manner around a central fountain. However, the roses and scented herbs that once filled the box-lined beds have been replaced by sheets of clear water. The effect of this imaginative transformation is quite delightful. Narrow paths run between the beautifully clipped hedges, and the composition is completed by a semicircular cypress arcade.

To the west, the villa overlooks a wide terrace bounded by a wall decorated with charming statues of dogs entwined with roses. Standing on the terrace, the cool breeze and the scent of the roses can be enjoyed along with the magnificent view of Florence shimmering in the heat below.

NEAREST MAJOR TOWN Lucca

MAIN FEATURES fine Baroque garden, green theatre, water staircase, *giochi d'acqua*, extravagant topiary

PRE-BOOKING no

OWNER Contessa Grazini Gardi

ADDRESS Via di Castello, 1-51014 Collodi

LOCATION Collodi is c. 17 kilometres north-east of Lucca on the ss435 to Montecatini Terme. It is signposted off the road 15 kilometres from Lucca, and the garden is easily found in the centre of the village

OPEN February to November, daily, 9.00–13.00, 15.00–sunset; note that the villa has separate opening hours

ADMISSION L10,000, children L6000

WHEELCHAIRS only in lower garden

REFRESHMENTS bar and light meals

LAVATORIES yes

The Garzoni family originated in Pescia, in the medieval Florentine Republic. Its political affiliations were such that the family became exiles on the death of Castruccio Castracani, Lord of Lucca, who led his troops to victory against the Florentines in 1325. The Garzoni sought refuge in Lucca, which soon became the family's home.

During the early years of the seventeenth century the family bought the old castle of Collodi, whose fortifications were torn down to make way for a new villa. A print of 1633 shows the new building without its garden. In 1652, Francesco Sbarra wrote *The Splendours of Collodi*, a poem which suggests that the garden was finished by this date.

The site had been ideal for a castle but as the setting for a handsome villa with extensive gardens it posed many problems. The new building stood on the edge of a cliff, making it impossible to lay out a garden in front of it. To the rear, the space was occupied by the medieval houses of the village, which had once clustered around the castle walls. The anonymous architect built a bridge to span the gorge to the east of the villa, so linking the house to the steep slope beyond the gorge. The garden was then laid out on the slope and the level ground below it.

In 1786 Ottavio Diodati, an architect and editor of a local edition of the French encyclopaedia, was employed to embellish the existing design. It is to him that we owe the terracotta statues, the *giochi d'acqua* and the green theatre.

Garzoni is one of the most spectacular Baroque gardens in Italy. It is flamboyant, humorous, detailed, colourful and decorative, and in the context of the subdued and subtle nature of Tuscan garden design it is unique. The Baroque desire to astonish has overcome a more typically Tuscan desire for intimate spaces in the garden.

The villa belonged to the Garzoni family until the beginning of this century. When the last Garzoni heir died the property changed hands many times before it was bought in 1945 by the late husband of the present owner.

A wooden door set into the high boundary wall serves as the visitors' entrance to the gardens, while the villa is perched high on the cliff above. Before leaving the busy village street and entering the strange Baroque world of the garden you must wait for one of the six gardeners to answer the old brass bell. As you enter the full extent of the design, culminating in the spectacular water staircase, is immediately visible. The main body of the garden is a circular space enclosed by yew tunnels or *berceaux*. The considerable height of the hedges and their strange, undulating form create the impression that the garden is encircled by a vast coronet. A series of balustraded steps and terraces lead up to the base of the massive water staircase that climbs the hill beyond. This striking and simple design is overlaid by a wealth of detail and colour.

The lower garden is a green menagerie. A peacock, dinosaur and elephant are among the topiary figures that stand about in it. Real swans swim in Diodati's two circular fountains, and cages of exotic game birds stand in the shade of the *berceaux* which form a sheltered walk that runs around the perimeter of the garden. The swirling arabesques of *parterres de broderie* create the foreground of the lower garden. The simple rectangular parterres that lie beyond them are planted with brightly coloured annuals, arranged to create complex geometric patterns. On the gentle slope above the plants give way to coloured pebbles forming the Garzoni family crest.

Three sets of balustraded steps link the lower garden to the base of the water staircase and to a network of paths running along the wooded slope towards the villa. The retaining wall at each level of the staircase is decorated with mosaics. The balustrades and strange little monkeys that adorn them are of terracotta. Like all the terracotta figures in the garden, the monkeys were Diodati's idea. Pots of trailing geranium stand on the balustrade, adding yet more colour to the scene.

Diodati installed *giochi d'acqua* in the magnificent grotto set in the retaining wall of the second flight of steps. The unwary might have been trapped by a wall of spray issuing from the step at the entrance. Additional jets sprang from the roof, walls and statue of Neptune. Standing perfectly still was the only way to avoid a soaking. Today, the gardener can be asked to demonstrate these *giochi d'acqua*.

The first terrace extends beyond the steps into an area known as the Viale degli Imperatori, named after the terracotta busts of Roman emperors that stand against the retaining wall. Diodati's green theatre, sadly neglected, lies at one end of the terrace. It is enclosed by hedges of box and yew. Gryphons holding *flambeaux* serve as footlights, and

statues of Tragedy and Comedy stand to either side of the raked stage. There are charming terracotta shell seats in the auditorium.

The double water staircase climbs the rough hillside above the steps and terraces, cutting through the bosco on either side. It is the climax of the garden and creates a transition from the cultivated areas to the wild. The staircase was originally fed by a spring that ran down the hill above the garden. Up to 400 barrels of crystal-clear water ran down the steps each hour and went on to feed the pools below. This system has been replaced by a motorised pump which draws water up.

William Beckford, the English antiquarian and eccentric, visited Garzoni at the end of the eighteenth century. His account gives a vivid image of the original force and effect of the water: 'the sun broke from the clouds, and lighted up the green of the vegetation; at the same time spangling the waters which pour copiously down a succession of rocky terraces. … The streams issue from a chasm in the cliff surrounded by cypresses, which conceal by their thick branches a pavilion with baths. Above rises a colossal statue of Fame, boldly carved, and in the very act of starting from the precipices. A narrow path leads up to the feet of the goddess, on which I reclined, while a vast column of water, arching over my head, fell without even wetting me with its spray, into the depths below'.

Fame was another of Diodati's innovations. Originally two cypresses served to stop the eye at the head of the staircase. The two statues below Fame on the staircase represent Lucca and Florence. The 'pavilion with baths' still stands at the head of the staircase, in easy reach of the villa. It has been closed to the public for several years and is falling into dereliction. There were once two magnificent marble baths, dressing rooms and a discreetly screened musicians gallery inside. It is said that the bathers listened to arias by Luigi Boccherini, a native of Lucca. Screens were also placed between the baths, allowing bathers to wash in private while continuing their conversations. As late as 1920 visitors described the sofas, which were still upholstered in their original faded silks, designed to match the white, blue and gold decoration of the walls.

Steep paths lead through the *bosco* to each side of the staircase. A dwarf, a Turk and a wild boar are among the terracotta figures beneath the trees. Many figures are badly damaged. Beyond the *bosco* to the left is the covered bridge that spans the gorge between the garden and villa. The bridge used to contain the controls for the *giochi d'acqua* at the centre of the maze laid out below it. The bridge itself was also riddled with water jets. The air of neglect and impending dereliction was particularly strong in this part of the garden when we visited, but a major programme of restoration is currently underway.

The terrace in front of the villa is closed to the public. Ducks and geese, kept to ward off snakes, live in the pavilions to either side of it. A beautiful Rococo summerhouse stands beyond the main building.

NEAREST MAJOR TOWN Siena
MAIN FEATURES simple garden in a rural setting, fine eighteenth-century green theatre
PRE-BOOKING yes
OWNER Bianchi-Bandinelli family
ADDRESS I-53010 Pianella; tel. +39 (0)577 356879)
LOCATION Geggiano is c. 8 kilometres north-east of Siena. Follow the SS408 from Siena for c. 5 kilometres. After Ponte al Bozzone turn left, following the sign for Villa Geggiano. The unsurfaced road continues for c. 1.5 kilometres, before becoming the entrance avenue to the villa
OPEN all year; only by appointment by letter or telephone
ADMISSION L20,000
WHEELCHAIRS yes
REFRESHMENTS wine and oil tasting, snack included
LAVATORIES yes

When the Bandinelli acquired Geggiano in the mid-sixteenth century it was a simple country villa with two medieval towers. It was not till 1780 that it was rebuilt in its present form. The loggia added to the first floor has since been closed, but in all other respects the villa is virtually unchanged, both inside and out. The walled garden and green theatre date from the same period.

Alfieri, the famous Piedmontese playwright, spent a good deal of time at Geggiano. In 1783, the first edition of his tragedies was published in Siena, and the plays were staged in the green theatre.

During the Second World War the villa became a refuge for Ranuccio Bandinelli's friends, most of whom were painters, poets and writers, many of them Jewish. In 1944, Bandinelli forestalled a German attempt to make a minefield out of the gardens by producing a letter from Kesselring, which he had actually removed from the front door of another building. The letter forbade the destruction of the villa on

account of its historic importance. When he was cross-questioned, Bandinelli was quick to substitute Goethe's name for Alfieri's, and to claim that it was one of his plays that had its première there.

A curved avenue of cypresses marks the road to Geggiano. Beyond the avenue it is enclosed by hedges clipped in an impressive variety of geometric shapes. The road then passes through a small *bosco* before arriving at one of the six ornamental gates set in the garden wall. Many of the stone and terracotta figures that decorate the wall have been broken, but the grimacing stone monkeys that stand above the lemon garden are a memorable sight.

The green theatre lies opposite the villa. The raised stage is faced with brick, and dilapidated brick arches stand on either side of it. They were originally decorated with the crests of the Chigi-Zondadari and the Bianchi-Bandinelli, commemorating a marriage between the two families. A Maltese sculptor called Bosio executed the statues of Comedy and Tragedy that stand in the niches. The stage is enclosed by a cypress hedge, which allowed the actors to move behind the scenes without being spotted by the audience. Clipped laurel forms the wings, and a single cypress creates a focus for the backdrop.

The lemon garden creates a delightful contrast with the somewhat dilapidated air of the theatre and its surroundings. The lemons stand on each side of a gravel path. The well-tended beds of vegetables and cutting flowers that lie beyond them must be the pride and joy of the single gardener employed to tend the grounds. At the far end of the garden is an enormous semicircular cistern.

tuscany (toscana)

NEAREST MAJOR TOWN Siena
MAIN FEATURES sixteenth-century gardens
PRE-BOOKING no
OWNER Comune di San Quirico
ADDRESS Piazza della Libertà, I-53027 San Quirico d'Orcia
LOCATION San Quirico is 40 kilometres south-east of Siena on the ss2, the old road to Rome. The gardens are easily found in the centre of town
OPEN all year, dawn to dusk. In summer the garden is open in the evening and is illuminated
ADMISSION free
WHEELCHAIRS no
REFRESHMENTS no
LAVATORIES no

It is said that Cosimo I de'Medici awarded the site of the ruined citadel of San Quirico to Diomede Leoni, a loyal Medici supporter and governor of the town to commemorate the cessation of hostilities between Florence and Siena. In 1581 the Governor of Siena wrote to Francesco I de'Medici describing how Leoni was transforming the site into a walled garden and had already restored the fortifications at his own considerable expense. It was already known as the 'Horti Leonini'; as with the Roman 'Horti Farnesiani', the use of *hortus* in the name indicates its importance.

The garden has always been public and it is thought that it was intended for the use of the many pilgrims who used to pass along the road to Rome, a fact suggested by the various wall-plaques with inscriptions such as 'Astonish yourself with the splendour, smoke and noise of Rome' and 'Exhausted by the effort of pilgrimage we have returned to our own hearths'.

A tall medieval tower originally stood in the upper garden. For centuries both the symbol and the pride of San Quirico, it was destroyed by German soldiers in 1944. The garden was later owned

by the Chigi-Zondadari; it now belongs to the Comune di San Quirico.

The garden is divided into two sections by a *bosco* of ilex. Only the lower garden survives intact, and it is not known what form the upper garden once had. Entry is from the piazza under an arch formed by two ancient ilexes. The garden plan is one of simple but perfect geometry. Immaculately clipped double box hedges in the form of a star cover the whole area. In the centre is a statue of Cosimo III de'Medici by Giuseppe Mazzuoli (1688), which is a recent addition, having been brought here in 1951 from the Palazzo Chigi in San Quirico. There is a small bed of roses; this is a predominantly green garden, and its perfect symmetry and unity of colour make it an unusually tranquil place.

Steps lead from the lower garden up through the *bosco*. The upper garden is now rough grass surrounded by ilex, but there is a fine view of the Val d'Orcia from the surrounding walls.

NEAREST MAJOR TOWN Florence

MAIN FEATURES important sixteenth-century Medici garden

PRE-BOOKING no

OWNER the State

ADDRESS Via di Castello, loc. Castello, 1-50141 Florence; tel.+39 (0)55 454791

LOCATION northern suburbs of Florence. From central Florence follow signs for Sesto Fiorentino until Castello is signposted to the right.

The villa is signposted to the right shortly afterwards

OPEN Tuesday to Sunday, November to February, 9.00–16.30; March and April, 9.00–17.30; May to October, 9.00–19.30

ADMISSION L4000, garden only (includes entrance to Villa Medicea della Petraia; page 199)

WHEELCHAIRS yes, with assistance

REFRESHMENTS no

LAVATORIES yes

Villa Medicea di Castello was acquired by Lorenzo di Pierfrancesco de'Medici in 1477. On his death it passed to Giovanni delle Bande Nere, who was the Grand Duke Cosimo 1's father. Cosimo became the first Grand Duke of Tuscany in 1537. The following year he decided to replace the existing layout at Castello with a new garden reflecting the magnificence of the Medici. It is said he asked Benedetto Varchi to plan it for him, a man best known as a historian and, it seems, likely responsible for the iconography of the garden, while Niccolò Tribolo took practical responsibility for the realisation of his ideas.

In 1549 Tribolo accepted the additional task of designing the Boboli Gardens for Cosimo (page 147). He died the following year, and his role at Castello was taken on by Bernado Buontalenti. Bartolommeo Ammanati and Giambologna both contributed sculptures.

Cosimo died in 1574, and he probably spent the last years of his life at Castello in the company of his second wife, Camilla Martelli.

tuscany (toscana)

The biographer Giorgio Vasari visited Castello in 1580 and described it as 'the most rich, magnificent and ornamental garden in Europe'. He also referred to a mulberry avenue flanked by canals that was to have run down the hill in front of the villa, linking it to the Arno. Sadly, this part of the grandiose plan was never realised.

At the end of the sixteenth century Castello was included in a series of lunettes by Giusto Utens. Here the structure of the garden is instantly recognisable, although the details are changed.

Like so many of the early Tuscan villas, Castello was built next to the road. The forecourt, which was adorned with two oblong fish-pools, was a setting for games and tournaments. The pools were filled in at the end of the eighteenth century, and the space is now used as a car park.

Giardini segreti were laid out on either side of the villa. According to Vasari, the one to the west was planted with 'strange herbs'. These may have been the medicinal herbs that Cosimo imported from America. Michel de Montaigne visited Castello in 1580 and was delighted by a magnificent tree house in the garden east of the villa. Both of the *giardini segreti* were lost during the eighteenth century.

The main body of the garden has always been enclosed by high walls, making it resemble a medieval *hortus conclusus*. Vasari was delighted by the espaliered pomegranate and bitter orange that grew against the wall, and the *berceaux* of scented cedar, cypress, olive and orange that shaded the paths. Tribolo built two fountains. The first stood close to the villa and was decorated with Ammanati's bronze of *Hercules Wrestling with Antaeus*. The other was surmounted by Giambologna's statue of Florence wringing water from her hair, and stood in the middle of a labyrinthine *bosco* of cypress, myrtle and laurel that created a focus at the centre of the garden. The fountain was moved to Petraia in 1760, the *bosco* cut down and the Hercules fountain shifted to the centre of the garden. The eastern portion of the garden, which Tribolo had laid out as an enclosed orchard with a pavilion, was destroyed at the same time and replaced with an area of 'English' woodland.

Castello was one of the first Italian gardens to be built around an iconographical theme. Every statue and fountain was designed to contribute to Varchi's complex programme that mirrored the achieve-

ments of Cosimo I and celebrated the establishment of the Medici as
an absolute monarchy. Part of Varchi's plan was never realised, and its
core was destroyed when the Florence fountain was removed. However, it is still possible to piece together his scheme. The lower garden
was seen as the lush and prosperous plain of Florence, presided over
by Florence herself, who stood at its centre. Varchi originally intended
that the little bosco should be peopled by statues representing the
Medici virtues of justice, piety, nobility, valour and generosity.
Although this part of the scheme was never realised, the Hercules
Wrestling with Antaeus was to be read as the victory of virtue over vice.
The water in which Florence bathes flows from the statue of Apennine
on the upper terrace. It then descends through the wall fountains to
either side of the grotto, which represent the rivers Arno and
Mugnone. Inside the grotto Cosimo is portrayed as the powerful uni-
corn, symbol of peace and purity.

Castello remained in the hands of the Medici till 1743, when the
family became extinct, and their property passed to the House of Lorraine. After the Unification of Italy it became State property. Over the
past decade the garden has been beautifully restored.

The gardens of Castello are laid out on a gentle slope behind the
villa. The lower garden is completely enclosed by walls and is flanked
to the east by an area of 'English' woodland.

Castello merits a visit on account of its important history, famous
grotto and magnificent collection of citrus fruit trees. However, visitors should be prepared for the bleak prospect of the lower parterre
garden. Tribolo's design has been destroyed by the loss of the little
bosco that once stood at its centre. There are no longer any vertical features to relieve the monotony of the parterres. A low wall and a flight

of shallow steps divides the parterres from the lemon garden. The Medici had always made a hobby of gardening, and like so many illustrious families they delighted in the collection and cultivation of citrus fruits. They were particularly interested in *bizzarie*, or 'bizarres', created by careful grafting. In this way multicoloured fruits, fruits with corrugated skins and others which resembled breasts, horns and buttocks were produced. These strange objects were offered as a precious gift to visitors and exchanged with other enthusiasts. Citrus flowers were sometimes dried and ground to a powder, which was added to food as a seasoning and to wine as a kind of preservative.

Visitors can still see 600 different varieties of citrus at Castello, with some trees being 200 years old. Originally each pot was carefully labelled but over the years many of the labels have been lost, and even the experts have found it difficult to identify every plant. The magnificent collection narrowly escaped destruction during the unusually cold winter of 1985, when the plants were saved by the head gardener, who rose in the night to light fires in the *limonaia*.

Tribolo's famous grotto is at the centre of the retaining wall behind the lemon garden. Its roof is decorated with elaborate shellwork and tufa, which takes the form of masks, Florentine lilies and arabesques. *Giochi d'acqua* are concealed in the mosaic floor, and pink and white marble basins encrusted with sea creatures adorn the walls. Water pours in the basins from the mouths and beaks of an extraordinary collection of animals and birds carved from a variety of appropriately coloured stones and adorned with real antlers and tusks. There are oxen and goats, a stag and wild boar, a camel, cat and elephant, to name but a few, and each relates in some way to a member of the Medici. The ram was the chosen symbol of Francesco, the goat symbolises Cosimo, the giraffe and dromedary relate to gifts given to Lorenzo by the Sultan of Egypt, while the elephant is a portrait of Hanno, which was given to the Medici Pope Leo x by the King of Portugal in 1514.

Two flights of steps lead up from the lemon garden to the upper terrace, where 'Appenino' stands shivering at the centre of his pool. The bearded face and naked torso of Ammanati's statue rise out of the long grass. Drops of water run in rivulets down his beard, giving the impression that Apennine is sobbing with cold.

NEAREST MAJOR TOWN Florence
MAIN FEATURES sixteenth-century
Medici villa
PRE-BOOKING no
OWNER the State
ADDRESS Via della Petraia 40,
loc. Castello, I-50141 Florence;
tel. +39 (0)55 452691
LOCATION northern suburbs of
Florence. From central Florence follow
signs for Sesto Fiorentino until
Castello is signposted to the right.
The villa is signposted to the right

shortly afterwards. The bus can also
be taken from the railway station
OPEN Tuesday to Sunday, November to
February, 9.00–16.30; March and
April, 9.00–17.30; May to October
9.00–19.30; closed national holidays.
Villa open daily, 9.00–13.30
ADMISSION L4000 (includes entrance to
Villa Medicea di Castello; page 193)
WHEELCHAIRS no
REFRESHMENTS no
LAVATORIES yes

The land of the Villa Medicea della Petraia originally belonged to the Palla di Noferi degli Strozzi, whose fortress had stood there since the early fourteenth century. In 1427 it was confiscated by Cosimo de'Medici the Elder, and sold to the Salutati family. In 1568 Cosimo 1 de'Medici bought it back to give to his second son Ferdinando who, having been made a cardinal at the age of 15, was living in the Villa Medici in Rome. In 1589 Ferdinando became Grand Duke by the death of his elder brother. He immediately commissioned Bernado Buontalenti for a villa and gardens at Petraia. The work was complete by 1595. The villa was built on the foundations of the ancient castle, but it retained its tall keep.

The design of the garden has changed and it is fortunate that it was recorded in a painting by Giusto Utens in 1599. It is the lowest of its three terraces that has changed out of all recognition. Buontalenti

tuscany (toscana)

chose to lay it out with *berceaux* forming two large ovals. In the centre of each was another circular *berceau* containing a simple fountain. Paths intersected in the middle of each circle, forming an elegantly symmetrical plan. The spaces inside each oval were planted with fruit trees.

As early as 1609, the year of Ferdinand's death, there is a note referring to work undertaken at Petraia 'to divide it up in the French manner'. At least some of this work was carried out by Giulio Parigi, who added the central fountain on the lower terrace. In 1760 the Fountain of Venus was brought from Castello (page 193) and installed on the upper terrace.

In 1865 Florence became the temporary capital of Italy, and Petraia was made a royal residence. Vittorio Emanuele II and his second wife Countess Mirafiori spent much time here, often dining on a platform set into an ancient ilex on the upper terrace. Flowerbeds were laid everywhere to suit nineteenth-century taste, thus removing the last traces of the original planting.

It is better to ignore the tempting lower entrance to the garden and to proceed up the steep cobbled lane to the villa. From the dark cypress woods that cover the hill above, a stream flows over a moss-covered cascade into a pool situated opposite the façade of the villa. A door in the wall to the right leads to the lemon garden on the upper terrace. The centrepiece is formed by Tribolo's fountain decorated with Giambologna's statue of Florence, brought here, like the Fountain of Venus in the eighteenth century, from Castello.

This terrace once commanded a fine view of the Arno valley with Florence and the surrounding hills. It is now sadly marred by industrial development, and the air is hazy with pollution. However, from the south-east corner of the lemon garden, where there is a small nineteenth-century loggia, there is still a good view of the city framed by trees. It can still be seen how villa and garden were situated in accordance with Leon Battista Alberti's ideals, overlooking 'the city … or a great plain and familiar hills and mountains'.

Immediately below the upper terrace there is a long *peschiera* parallel to the front of the villa. It is reached by a flight of flower-lined steps at each end. Jets of water are set along its length, and the edge is lined with pots of trailing geranium.

tuscany (toscana)

A central flight of steps leads down to the third and lowest level which slopes down to a row of poplars that lines the southern boundary of the garden. The level is covered with geometrical parterres filled with flowers and in the centre is a graceful fountain surrounded by stone benches and a circular box hedge. To left and right of the fountain are *boschetti* of ilex, probably planted during the seventeenth century to replace Buontalenti's *berceaux*. The exit, which lies to the right through the trees, passes an area of rough grass filled with poppies blazing against a background of black ilex bark.

NEAREST MAJOR TOWN Florence
MAIN FEATURES fifteenth-century
Medici garden with magnificent views
PRE-BOOKING strictly by appointment
with the owner
OWNER Signora Anna Mazzini
ADDRESS Via Vecchia Fiesolana,
1-50014 Fiesole; tel. +39 (0)55 59417
LOCATION Via Vecchia Fiesolana is a
steep hill running west from Piazza
Mino in Fiesole. The villa is on the left
at the end of a long wall. Ring the bell
on the tiny door set in the wall of the
villa. Note that the door is painted the
same colour as the wall, and so is
easily missed
OPEN Monday to Saturday, mornings
only
ADMISSION L10,000, for cancer
research
WHEELCHAIRS no
REFRESHMENTS no
LAVATORIES no

Cosimo the Elder bought the villa, known as Belcanto, from the Bardi in 1458. He employed Michelozzo Michelozzi to rebuild it, intending to give the new house to Giovanni, his only son. Construction was arduous and expensive, as foundations had to be sunk in the precipitous hillside. When the building was finished Michelozzo laid out gardens around it, just as he had done at Cosimo's villas in Cafaggiolo and Careggi. It is said that Cosimo was doubtful about the charm of the new garden for he took no pleasure in the magnificent view, preferring his own country retreat at Cafaggiolo, where everything he could see from the windows was his possession.

The villa and its garden were complete by 1461. Two years later Giovanni, who was immensely fat, died of a heart attack and Cosimo took no further interest in the place.

Villa Medici found favour again under Lorenzo il Magnifico, who took Cosimo's place as a leader among the humanists of the day, and as a member of the Platonist Academy. He was delighted by the garden, which he saw as a perfect setting for learned discussions, poetry readings and private meditation. It is said that the members of the Pazzi conspiracy originally planned to murder Lorenzo and his brother Giuliano at a banquet to be given at the villa. This proved to be one of numerous false alarms for the banquet was cancelled when Giuliano injured his leg in a hunting accident; the murderers finally resorted to attacking the brothers during High Mass in the Duomo in Florence.

Cosimo III sold the villa in 1671 to Vincenzo di Cosimo Serra, an act that marked the beginning of a series of different ownerships. In 1772 it was bought by the Duchess of Orford, Sir Robert Walpole's eccentric widow. The villa was almost completely rebuilt by the Buoninsegni family who bought it in 1780. During the nineteenth century it was known as Villa Spence, having been bought by Willian Blundell Spence, the English painter and collector. In 1911 Lady Sybil Cutting bought the property and restored the lower garden with the help of the architect Cecil Pinsent. Her daughter Iris Origo grew up there, and has written about her childhood at the villa in her autobiography *Images and Shadows*.

Despite the virtual rebuilding of the villa during the eighteenth century, Michelozzo's garden escaped radical transformation. It is quite unlike the simple, almost medieval gardens he designed for Cosimo's villas at Careggi and Cafaggiolo. Here, the precipitous hillside was cut in terraces set out to embrace the magnificent view. Despite this radical departure from the tradition of the enclosed garden, Michelozzo did not consider it necessary to link the different levels of his design. Had he been working a century later he would no doubt have built

ramps or steps between the terraces. As it is, the lower terrace can only be reached by a circuitous path that runs down from the entrance to the upper garden, which seems to hang in space above the view, stretching across the valley. The only boundary is a low brick wall, decorated with terracotta pots of red geranium. On the other side the terrace is completely screened from the road by a high wall, said to be of Etruscan origin. To the east the garden it is enclosed by the delicately frescoed loggia of the villa, and to the west by an elaborately decorated wall.

Much of the terrace is occupied by lawns divided by paths and shaded by ancient paulownia. The paths are lined by pots of lemon, which are carried into the *limonaia* in the corner of the garden each autumn. The narrow terrace that lies against the boundary wall is thought to date from the eighteenth century and is planted with climbing roses grown in swags or festoons in the French manner.

The pretty nymphaeum at the far end of the garden is decorated with *spugne* and elaborate pebble mosaic, which is made of red, black, white and cream-coloured pebbles and which extends on to the wall that flanks the main entrance.

On the other side of the entrance is a beautiful seventeenth-century loggia. It is open on one side to the garden and on the other has a magnificent view across the valley. The back wall is decorated with a *trompe-l'oeil* painting which is a mirror image of the garden. The same mosaic of shells, pebbles and *spugne* adorn the outer walls. At the back, the initials 'vs' for Vincenzo Serra are set in the mosaic.

The ilexes that grow above the main drive have leant right over, creating a kind of tunnel. Steps lead up through the trees to a second terrace above the *limonaia*. This part of the garden has been virtually

tuscany (toscana)

abandoned. An overgrown cypress avenue extends beyond the remains of an elaborate grotto set into the side of the hill.

The lower garden was completely redesigned by Cecil Pinsent in 1911, but the magnificent, raised pergola running along the bottom of the retaining wall may have been a part of the original layout. There is a similar pergola at Cosimo's villa in Cafaggiolo. Ancient wisteria entwines the balustrades of the steps that lead down from the centre of the pergola. Pinsent bowed to the splendour of the setting by creating the simplest of designs. Lawns, parterres and pots of lemon are arranged around a circular fountain. Like the rest of the garden, the lower terrace is meticulously maintained by a single gardener.

The last of Michelozzo's terrace gardens lies on the other side of the villa and can be reached by walking to the end of the pergola and crossing the enclosed area below the building. Every detail of his original design has survived in this secluded hanging garden. Green parterres divided by gravel paths are arranged around a circular fountain. The shady stone seats set in the wall of the villa may have been used by Lorenzo and his friends from the Platonist Academy.

NEAREST MAJOR TOWN Lucca
MAIN FEATURES fine seventeenth-century garden rooms with green theatre, water theatre
PRE-BOOKING no
OWNER Conti Pecci-Blunt
ADDRESS Via Villa Reale, I-55014 Marlia; tel. +39 (0)583 30108/30009
LOCATION Marlia is 10 kilometres north-east of Lucca. Take the SS435 for Montecatini Terme. After 7 kilometres turn left for Marlia and follow signs for Villa Reale. At the traffic lights turn right following a small sign to Ville Lucchese. Turn left at the war memorial and follow the garden wall to the main entrance
OPEN (garden only) March to November, Tuesday to Sunday, guided tours at 10.00, 11.00, 15.00, 16.00, 17.00, 18.00. Groups can be accommodated on Mondays by arrangement
ADMISSION L6000
WHEELCHAIRS no
REFRESHMENTS no
LAVATORIES no

Villa Reale takes its name from the royal connections of two of its nineteenth-century owners. Since the fourteenth century the land had belonged to the Orsetti family and during the sixteenth century its defensive fortress was demolished and a villa erected in its place. The gardens were laid out in the following century. The designer is not known.

In 1805 Napoleon crowned himself King of Italy. The following year he created his sister, Elise Bonaparte, Princess of Lucca and Piombino. On her elevation she compelled the Orsetti to sell their ancient home, and set about transforming it into a Ruritanian court-in-miniature. Her husband, Count Felice Bacciocchi, became Minister of War and Commander of the tiny Luccan army. Nicolò Paganini was appointed the Royal Director of Music. Elise immediately set to work

on the property, expropriating so much land from her neighbours that it doubled in size. The lovely Grotto of Pan, previously in somebody else's garden, was included at this time. The Neo-classical gatehouses were also added during this period.

In 1811 Elise started to transform the garden, turning much of it into an 'English' park, and adding a huge ornamental lake. The seventeenth-century garden rooms were probably saved by Napoleon's downfall in 1814. Elise was evicted, and the villa passed to its next resident, the erstwhile Duchess of Parma, the Bourbon Maria Luisa. She received the Duchy of Lucca in compensation for losing Parma, by a decision of the Congress of Vienna. They had decided to give the Duchy of Parma to Napoleon's wife Marie-Louise (daughter of the Austrian Emperor). Maria Luisa was succeeded by her son, who in 1847 ceded the Duchy to Tuscany. Villa Reale was later given to the widow of the Prince of Capua, whose family owned it till 1923. It was then bought by Count and Countess Pecci-Blunt, who restored it and added a small modern garden. It is still owned by their family.

The seventeenth-century garden is reached by crossing the broad *manège* that sweeps down from the villa to the lake. Statues are set in the banks of rhododendron on either side. Though it looks as though it had been cleared during the nineteenth-century alterations, the *manège* is in fact an entirely traditional feature and is recorded in the earliest engravings of this garden. On the far side a short alley through the ilex woods leads to a gate in the lemon garden. This is the first in a series of garden rooms made to feel successively more enclosed. At the northern end of this 'room' is a rectangular balustraded pool overlooked by two bearded river gods, Arno and Serchio, and a nymphaeum containing Leda and the Swan. Real swans float on the pool, disturbing the reflections of the lemon trees lining the balustrade. The nymphaeum is mirrored by an apse at the far end of the garden.

To the east of the pool, wrought-iron gates between heavily rusticated columns open into a circular 'anteroom'. Steps lead up to a smaller circular pool from which rises a single, tall plume of water, brilliant against the background of dark yew and magnolia. The figures of the Four Seasons stand around the anteroom. Beyond, visible through

the spray, is the green theatre, perhaps the finest, though not the largest, in Italy. It is enclosed by 20-foot yew hedges, with windows and doors cut into them. Footlights, orchestra pit, prompter's box and seating are all cut from box or yew. Life-size terracotta *commedia dell'arte* figures stand in niches cut in the backdrop. The four gardeners clip all this, and the rest of the garden, by hand – it takes nearly three months a year.

There is a simple water theatre behind the villa with a semicircular pool filled from lion masks set around the wall behind it. A path runs around the top of the wall, backed by a high ilex hedge. The centrepiece is a grotto above the path containing a stepped cascade.

South of the lemon garden is the sixteenth-century Grotto of Pan, an unusual two-storey structure deep in the woods. The exterior is entirely covered with mosaic and *spugne*. The open ground-floor loggia has a marble bowl in the centre, filled with trailing geranium, while the ceiling is decorated with stone plants and flowers, and has a star in the middle of the ceiling from which water can spray. Terracotta urns overflowing with *spugne* stand in niches. The grotto has a domed ceiling and mosaic floor with figures of Pan and accompanying Tritons set in niches. On close inspection the jets set around the walls can be seen, for what must have been a deluge of spray.

NEAREST MAJOR TOWN Pisa
MAIN FEATURES the oldest botanical garden in Europe
PRE-BOOKING no
OWNER University of Pisa
ADDRESS Via Luca Ghini 5, I-56126 Pisa
LOCATION close to Piazza del Duomo, Pisa
OPEN Monday to Friday, 8.00–13.00, 14–17.30; Saturday, 8.00–13.00; closed Sunday and public holidays
ADMISSION free
WHEELCHAIRS yes
REFRESHMENTS no
LAVATORIES yes

The botanical garden of Pisa is the oldest in Europe, founded in 1543 by Luca Ghini, who also established the Giardino dei Semplici in Florence two years later. His patron in both cases was Cosimo I de'Medici. Its present site is not original, though it is still of some antiquity. The garden had to be moved twice in its first 50 years of existence and it was not until 1591 that a permanent location was found. The original purpose of such gardens was invariably to teach students the medicinal uses of plants, according to which uses plants were classified. At this time the medieval 'doctrine of signatures' was still generally in use; in other words, if a plant happened to resemble some part of the human anatomy then it must be of some benefit to that part. The walnut, for instance, was thought to help diseases of the brain. Ghini's successor in 1554 was Andrea Cesalpino, who was the first to classify plants instead by the characteristics of their fruits and seeds, thus laying the foundations of modern botany.

One of Ghini's first students, Lugi Squalerno, became the first director of the botanic garden at Padua (founded in 1545 and still the least altered of the three gardens). His name is thus directly associated with the rise of botanical knowledge in Europe. Ghini was awarded the

Chair of Botany at the University of Pisa by Cosimo de'Medici. The gardens have remained affiliated to the University ever since.

The layout of the garden is substantially changed since the sixteenth century. A plan of 1723 shows eight square beds in a regular grid pattern. Though these no longer exist, they are reflected by the present formal pattern of the beds in the 'Botany School' (bear left after entering the garden). Though it was only laid out 150 years ago, with its six small fountains and rectangular beds planted to teach plant relationships, it is possible to visualise how this garden must have functioned in its earliest years. Also in this area stands the oldest surviving building, the original Botanic Institute with its wonderful sixteenth-century façade decorated in shell work.

There are magnificent trees in the garden, including a *Ginkgo biloba* planted in 1787. The specialist guide (available in four languages) is recommended as it describes in detail the plants of greatest interest.

NEAREST MAJOR TOWN Siena

MAIN FEATURES small fifteenth-century hanging garden, wonderful views

PRE-BOOKING no

OWNER La Società Esecutori Pie Disposizione, Siena

ADDRESS Piazza Pio II, I-53026 Pienza; tel.: + 39 (0)578 748503

LOCATION Pienza is 50 kilometres south-east of Siena. From Siena take the SS2, the old road to Rome. After 40 kilometres turn left at San Quirico. The palazzo is to the right of the cathedral in the main piazza.

OPEN Tuesday to Sunday, 10.00–12.30, 16.00–19.00 (summer), 10.00–12.30, 15.00–18.00 (winter); closed 20 November to 7 December, 26 February to 8 March. Entrance to the garden is by request after the tour of the palazzo, though it can be seen from the loggia as part of the tour

ADMISSION L5000, groups L3500 each

WHEELCHAIRS yes (garden only)

REFRESHMENTS no

LAVATORIES no

This small but spectacular garden is one of the earliest to have survived almost unchanged since its creation. In 1458 Aeneas Silvius Piccolomini was elected to the papacy as Pius II. Shortly afterwards he conceived the ambitious plan of rebuilding as an ideal town the village where he was born, Corsignano, and renaming Pienza after himself. He turned first to Leon Battista Alberti, whose humanist ideals were close to his own. Alberti was not a practical architect, though a distinguished architectural theorist. He suggested commissioning Bernardo Rossellino, who had recently completed Palazzo Rucellai in Florence following Alberti's designs. The two had met in Rome in the 1450s when working on the unexecuted urban designs of Nicholas V.

Rossellino's brief was to draw up plans for the town and be responsible for the building of the Duomo and the palazzo, which stand next to each other in the central piazza. He quoted 18,000 ducats for the

project. The site was difficult, being little more than 4200 square metres on the edge of a cliff – the Duomo in fact is built out over the precipice. The ground was poor, and foundations for the palazzo were more than 30 metres deep. Several of the workmen are still there, buried when the hole collapsed.

By the completion of the work the cost had risen to more than 50,000 ducats. A law of the time (one that might usefully be revived) required that Rossellino should repay the difference. Pius, however, congratulated him and awarded a cloak of honour, saying that if Rossellino had quoted him the true cost, the money would never have been raised and Italy would have been deprived of these marvellous buildings. The trapeziodal piazza complex, with the Duomo and the palazzi of the Piccolomini, bishop and commune, is important for the history of urban planning and influenced Michelangelo's layout of the Capitoline Hill in Rome of about a century later.

The palazzo remained in the possession of the Piccolomini until the death of the last member of the family in 1978. Since then the property has been administered by a charitable trust.

Despite the problems of construction, Rossellino treated the spectacular site with an impressive boldness. The palazzo overlooks the whole of the Val d'Orcia and the garden lies in the tiny space between the palazzo and the cliff. On entering the square courtyard of the palazzo, the stairs to the *piano nobile* are on the right; immediately opposite is the garden entrance.

Having taken the tour of the palazzo, the garden is seen first from the loggia on the *piano nobile*. The view is breathtaking and is unchanged since Pius wrote about it more than 500 years ago: 'You look down into the valley of the Val d'Orcia, green fields and little hills covered with the season's growth, fields cultivated with fruit and vines, towns and castles and rocky precipices ... and Radicofani, gateway of the winter's sun'.

The garden lies at your feet, in effect a small garden room with four rectangular parterres and raised beds around the walls. On the edge of the cliff a wall provides shelter: it is pierced with three arches so that with one step it is possible to turn from the enclosed privacy of the garden to look out over the open countryside below. Both palazzo and garden are designed specifically for the enjoyment of the view, obeying the humanist injunction that the surrounding landscape should determine the form of the garden. This is a radical shift from the inward-looking medieval desire to exclude nature in all but its domesticated forms.

NEAREST MAJOR TOWN Florence

MAIN FEATURES twentieth-century Italianate garden, green theatre, fine collection of statues

PRE-BOOKING yes

OWNER New York University

ADDRESS Via Bolognese 120, La Pietra, Florence; tel.: + 39 (0)555 474448

LOCATION follow signs to the north for Bologna (SS65) from Piazza della Libertà. The entrance to the villa is on the right on a sharp bend 1.5 kilometres from the piazza

OPEN applications in writing only; permission normally granted only to those with special interest

ADMISSION L12,000

WHEELCHAIRS no

REFRESHMENTS no

LAVATORIES no

La Pietra was originally a castellated farmhouse, built at the beginning of the fifteenth century for the Macinghi family. Its name, 'the stone', derives from the milestone that used to mark its distance from the city gate of San Gallo. In 1460 the house was bought by Francesco Sassetti, a Ghibelline and a leading Florentine banker under both Cosimo de'Medici and his grandson Lorenzo. Under his ownership the villa was remodelled as a typical Renaissance palace. Sassetti lived there with his wife, Nera dei Corsi, and their ten children.

After Sassetti's death in 1491 the villa was bought by the Capponi family who have owned it for 300 years. It owes its Baroque exterior to Cardinal Luigi Capponi, who undertook substantial renovations during the seventeenth century. The Capponi coat of arms surmounted by a cardinal's hat still adorns the rear wall of the villa. It is thought that the Capponi commissioned Carlo Fontana to undertake the restructuring of the villa. The gatehouses were also added at this time.

The main garden was entirely destroyed when landscaped in the English manner during the nineteenth century. Only the walled garden

to the north of the house survived. It is now the lemon garden. In 1902 La Pietra was bought by Arthur and Hortense Acton. Two years later the process of 'Tuscanising' the garden began, the enormous project being continued by Harold after the death of his parents.

The property is entered by way of a dramatic cypress avenue that frames the house at its far end. The avenue runs for about 800 metres through the olive groves. The trees are under-planted with *Rosa chinensis* which is in flower almost continuously between March and November.

La Pietra is a triumphant synthesis. It combines the typically Tuscan idea of the highly structured, green garden with a powerful Edwardian Englishness. Massive hedges and elaborate topiary divide the site in a series of self-contained rooms, each with its own particular atmosphere. Many of the hedges have reached an immense height – 9 metres or more – and the numerous garden rooms give a strong sense of solitude and privacy. The play of sunlight and shade gives life to the deep greens of the enclosing hedges. This very Italianate idea is then overlaid with an intrinsically English abundance of flowering climbers. The staircases are draped with Dorothy Perkins rose, the pergola is a mass of *Rosa banksia* and the Corinthian peristyle drips wisteria. The combination of this abundance with the formality of the structure is profoundly beautiful.

The main garden is laid out on a series of broad terraces to the southeast of the house. The upper terrace has a stone balustrade ornamented with statues and busts. The garden resembles an enormous gallery, designed to display Arthur's important collection of statues. The statues serve as focal points among the network of intersecting paths. At least one hundred of them are by the Venetian sculptor Orazio Marinali who with his brothers, Francesco and Angelo, provided statues for Andrea Palladio's villas.

At the lowest level an opening in a screen of yew reveals the Greek peristyle laid out around a central fountain. Rings of box have been planted to echo the shape of the colonnade. The green theatre to the left of the peristyle is one of the garden's most memorable features. The stage is peopled by charming eighteenth-century Venetian figures attributed to Francesco Bonazza. Among them is a girl cradling a rabbit and a bevy of servants ready to offer flowers, fruit and hot chocolate to the audience. The wings and the footlights are cut from box.

North of the villa is a walled lemon garden, the only part of the garden to have survived the nineteenth century and largely unchanged since Cardinal Capponi enlarged it in 1690 and built the *limonaia*, which is ornamented with *rocaille* work and has busts along the cornice. The walls surrounding the garden are similarly decorated.

La Pietra is a difficult garden to classify. Its conscious theatricality is the antithesis of the Tuscan style. Arthur Acton drew his ideas from many periods of garden design and from all parts of Italy, but most of all from his own imagination. The result is a dream-like Italian garden.

NEAREST MAJOR TOWN Florence
MAIN FEATURES terraced garden designed on 'Renaissance' lines by Cecil Pinsent
PRE-BOOKING yes
OWNER Harvard University
ADDRESS Via di Vincigliata 26, 1-50014 Settignano
LOCATION Settignano is north-east of Florence. Follow Via Gabriele d'Annunzio out of Florence. Via Vincigliata is on the left of the road, just beyond Coverciano. The villa is on a sharp bend about 500 metres up the road
OPEN on written application to Harvard University at the villa
ADMISSION at the owner's discretion
WHEELCHAIRS no
REFRESHMENTS no
LAVATORIES no

I Tatti was built in 1563 as a simple farmhouse. It was later absorbed in the estate of La Vincigliata, the pseudo-medieval castle above Settignano. Bernard Berenson, the famous American art critic and collector, bought the villa with 40 acres of land, most of it planted with fir and cypress, on his marriage in 1905. The rough garden to the rear of the villa was little more than a few fruit trees planted on a steep slope.

Since the eighteenth century there had been a large expatriate community in and around Florence. At the time that Berenson bought I Tatti, numerous other foreigners, many of them English, were buying villas in the hills surrounding the city. Some villas had been empty for years and their gardens were derelict. Others had nineteenth-century *giardini all'inglese* in place of gardens. Ironically, the English were the first to reject the expanses of grass and woodland that this implied and restored their gardens in the Renaissance manner. The consequence of their efforts was the creation of a peculiarly English neo-Renaissance style. The architect Cecil Pinsent excelled in this field, and he was

employed to create at least 20 private gardens in Tuscany. In 1908 he was commissioned by Berenson to redesign the garden at I Tatti. The task took seven years.

Berenson lived at I Tatti for more than half a century and it became a meeting place for intellectuals from all over the world. His own description of his house was 'a library with some rooms attached'. When he died in 1959 he left villa and library to Harvard, his university. He and his wife are buried in the chapel beside the villa.

Pinsent created a Tuscan garden in miniature on the south-facing slope behind the villa. The site is cleverly divided by the old *limonaia*, which runs across the slope, effectively screening the lower garden to create two substantial garden rooms.

Pots of flowering geranium stand on the broad terrace outside the villa. The ground slopes down from the terrace towards the *limonaia*. A steep path creates the axis of the simple layout, which consists of a series of parterres arranged around four large persimmon trees. The central portion of the *limonaia* has been transformed into a covered terrace that overlooks the lower garden.

A double flight of steps runs down to the garden from the *limonaia*. A wall fountain set beneath the steps flows into a small pool. The lower garden is completely enclosed by hedges and has a series of narrow terraces cut into the hillside. Each terrace is marked by an immaculately clipped box hedge. Between the hedges low, geometric parterres are laid out against a background of neat gravel. By excluding flowers from this area Pinsent created his own version of the early Renaissance green garden. A flight of steps runs down from the pool, neatly balancing the horizontal lines of the terraces. The steps are decorated with charming pebble mosaics and are flanked by obelisks of clipped box. Like the wide hedges and parterres to either side of them, these obelisks represent Pinsent's own interpretation of the Italian Renaissance style. Opinion varies as to how successful this interpretation was. Many feel that Pinsent had absorbed the detail of Renaissance design without understanding its substance. They see his garden as something of a pastiche. Berenson was more than satisfied with Pinsent's work saying of the garden: 'I love it as much as one can love any object or complex of objects not human'.

A pool lies at the lowest level of the garden; beyond the view extends over open countryside. Berenson designed the cupola near the pool.

Mary Berenson was not enamoured of Pinsent's formal garden and commissioned Aubrey Waterfield to plant a woodland garden below the terraces. Waterfield, who was married to Janet Ross' niece, also planted the meadow surrounding the garden with narcissus, fritillary and anemone. The cypress avenue that runs through Mary's wood links the villa to the lower entrance. Berenson arranged for the planting to be tapered to increase the sense of perspective.

tuscany (toscana)

NEAREST MAJOR TOWN Lucca
MAIN FEATURES seventeenth-century sunken garden and pool set amid a nineteenth-century 'English' landscape garden in a rural setting
PRE-BOOKING no
OWNER Principe Colonna Torrigiani
ADDRESS I-55010 Camigliano; tel.: +39 (0)583 928008; fax.: (0)583 928041
LOCATION from the autostrada Firenze-Mare take the Capannori exit. Follow signs for Segromigno in Monte and then Camigliano. The villa is signposted from the village (do not be misled by signs for Villa Mansi)
OPEN March to October, Wednesday to Monday, 10.00–12.00, 15.00–sunset
ADMISSION garden and villa L12,000, garden only L7000, groups L5000 each, CHILDREN free
WHEELCHAIRS yes, with assistance
REFRESHMENTS no
LAVATORIES yes

The original villa was a simple structure built during the sixteenth century for the Buonvisi family. During the seventeenth century it passed to the Santini family and was known as Villa Santini. The change of ownership marked the beginning of the villa's period of grandeur. Marquis Niccolò Santini, who was Lucca's ambassador to the court of Louis XIV at Versailles, chose the villa as his summer residence and had it altered to suit his fashionable tastes. The simple exterior to the south was pulled down and replaced with an elaborate Mannerist façade. The villa is still the most spectacular example of the Mannerist style in Lucca. The design has been tentatively attributed to Muzio Oddi, an architect from Urbino who came to Lucca to design the city wall.

The French garden designer André Le Nôtre is said to have spent three days with Santini when on his way to Rome to visit the pope. During his stay he sketched a design for the gardens to be laid out around the villa; the principal themes of this design are depicted in the ceiling frescoes of the reception rooms. A plan of the original garden also hangs in the villa. It shows *broderie* parterres arranged around two large pools to the front of the building. To the rear, a fountain formed the focus of a second parterre garden. An oblong pool and a sunken garden were laid out to the east of the villa.

In 1816 Vittoria Santini married Guadagni Torrigiani. Shortly afterwards the gardens were uprooted for a fashionable 'English' park. Only the sunken Garden of Flora, built to the east of the villa in 1650, and the oblong pool above it survived.

A magnificent cypress avenue frames the entrance to the villa. A few cottages are arranged around a small courtyard outside its gates. To the left of the entrance is the village chapel with its Romanesque bell tower. The gateway to the villa is flanked by two stone piers crowned with vases and obelisks. The ornate Mannerist façade of the building rises beyond two irregular pools, which are the only remains of the original seventeenth-century parterre garden.

The original garden at Villa Torrigiani was built on the intimate, almost domestic, scale typical of Tuscan villas in the sixteenth and seventeenth centuries. The small, rectangular space of the sunken Garden of Flora would originally have been planted with aromatic herbs and it acts as a sun trap in winter. It is linked to the upper terrace by a graceful flight of balustraded steps, built in perfect proportion to the garden. An arch set in the retaining wall of the staircase contains a pool and a small grotto. A passage hung with stalactites runs behind the grotto and can be entered through the arch at the right-hand end of the retaining wall.

A path decorated with pebble mosaic leads directly from the staircase to the Temple of Flora at the far end of the garden. The path is rid-

dled with concealed water pipes. Like all the *giochi d'acqua* in the garden these are fed by a plentiful and powerful water supply. The water is collected in a large reservoir on the hillside above the garden. By orchestrating innumerable *giochi d'acqua*, the Marquis could have chased his unwary guests down into the garden from the upper terrace. Once there, they would find their return barred by a wall of spray and as they retreated down the path they would soon have discovered that there was no escape. Dripping and breathless, they might have sought shelter in the Temple of Flora, only to find that it was the climax of

their host's entertainment. The temple is really a magnificent, dripping grotto surmounted by a cupola. Statues of the four winds spout water from their mouths and additional jets are set into the tufa ceiling and mosaic floor. Flora stands on the cupola, with delicate wrought-iron flowers at her feet. The gardener is willing to demonstrate the *giochi d'acqua* in the temple, an enlightening experience for anyone unfamiliar with the robust nature of seventeenth-century humour. It was probably the *giochi d'acqua* that saved this part of the garden from modernisation. The Italians have found water tricks irresistable ever since their invention by the ancient Romans.

The graceful oblong pool above the sunken garden is also part of the original design. It is shaded by trees and decorated with pots of lemon and statues. Water pours from the mouths of two masks set in the balustrade at the far end. Beyond the pool paths lead through the *bosco* to views of the open countryside beyond.

NEAREST MAJOR TOWN Siena
MAIN FEATURES sixteenth-century terrace garden
PRE-BOOKING yes
OWNER Marchesi Chigi Zondadari
ADDRESS Via Vicobello 12, Vico Alto, I-53100 Siena; tel.: +39 (0)564 933500
LOCATION Vicobello is north of Siena. Leave the town centre on the Via Garibaldi. Turn right over the railway at the traffic lights just before the station, following signs for 'Camping'. Follow the dual carriageway for about 500 metres. Turn left immediately before going under a bridge (to do this you have to turn round and come back down the other side of the dual carriageway). The avenue to Vicobello is the first turning to the left, with the villa on the left on the hill
OPEN by appointment by letter or telephone
ADMISSION free
WHEELCHAIRS no
REFRESHMENTS no
LAVATORIES no

Vicobello was designed for the Chigi family by Baldassare Peruzzi in 1576. When building work finished in 1580 Peruzzi laid out gardens on the steep, south-facing hillside overlooking Siena.

Much of the original layout was destroyed during the eighteenth century when an additional terrace was built beyond the boundary wall below the villa. However, it is known that the lemon garden with its delightful exedral apse was part of Peruzzi's design.

When seen from Siena, the garden was said to resemble the *sei monti*, or six mountains, of the Chigi family crest. It may be that Peruzzi's terraces, piled one above the other and decorated with arched *berceaux*, did resemble the crest's jelly mould form which can be seen all over the garden.

The existing layout at Vicobello is of the simplicity typical of Tuscan gardens. The terraces are linked by modest flights of steps, and

tuscany (toscana)

no attempt has been made to make architectural use of the sloping site. The villa, which still belongs to the Chigi, has been named a national monument.

Unlike so many villas of the sixteenth century, Vicobello does not form the focus of a grand entrance avenue. The road leading up from the gatehouse is flanked by limes, but it runs parallel to the villa and continues beyond the inconspicuous gateway that serves as the principal entrance. The gateway is marked by a small, semicircular piazza that extends to one side of the road. The wall enclosing is decorated with busts and is line with stone seats. Steps cut through the rows of square-topped ilexes that run across the hillside below. Below the trees is a level lawn bordered by an ilex hedge. It is thought that this originally served as a bowling green.

Once in the courtyard before the villa, the view through the arched gateway at ilexes frames a lovely view of hills and open country. The trees conceal the new hospital immediately below. The courtyard is enclosed on one side by the villa and on the other by a string of buildings that were once stables, servants' quarters, cellars and coach houses. A well stands between columns against the wall to one side of the gate. At its northern end the courtyard is bounded by a walled *bosco* laid out to either side of an avenue of plane and chestnut. A retaining wall isolates the area from the hillside below, this being a common security measure in those uncertain times.

The lemon garden at the other end of the courtyard is bounded by the *limonaia* and by clipped yew and box hedges. Peruzzi's beautiful apse is framed by cypresses on the far side of the garden. Its curving inner wall is decorated with niches, and two Roman busts stand either side of the roof, which has the ubiquitous family crest at the centre.

A path runs down the centre of the garden, and lemon trees of an incredible size adorn the *parterres* that lie either side of it. Their impressive terracotta pots are decorated with garlands. Some of the trees are more than 300 years old, yet their fruit is good – a single lemon is said to produce half a glass of juice.

Gateposts adorned with the family crest flank the entrance to the fruit garden on the terrace below. Some of the fruit trees stand in parterre beds, and others are espaliered against the brick wall of the upper terrace. Two oval fishpools with wide stone rims stand among the parterres at either end of the garden.

The narrow terrace below the fruit garden is shaded by a massive cedar planted in 1620. Azaleas fill the garden with a blaze of colour throughout the spring, and 20 different varieties of orchid hang in baskets from the trees.

A tunnel cuts through the boundary wall at the far end of the terrace and leads to the eighteenth-century flower garden. It is guarded at both ends by grotesques, and *spugne* adorn the walls. The greenhouse just inside the entrance was once a geological museum and contained specimens from all over Tuscany. Beds of brightly coloured annuals are arranged around the enormous ginkgo tree in the centre of the garden. A small balcony set in the retaining wall on the far side of the terrace gives a fine view of Siena.

Benevolent lions guard the steps that lead out of the flower garden. The Chigi crest fashioned out of topiary dominates the narrow terrace above. Another flight of steps leads up towards the villa. A fountain set into the retaining wall and decorated with stalactites serves as an overflow – it only plays when there is too much water in the cistern that lies beneath the upper terrace. The villa and family chapel are side by side on the upper terrace, which is adorned only with simple, circular beds of brightly flowering annuals.

emilia-romagna and le marche

Emilia-Romagna has a wide variety of climate and landscape, stretching as it does from the Apennine mountains to the River Po. Its name derives from the great Roman road that crosses it, the Via Aemilia.

Few gardens generally accessible to the public survive here. One has been selected in Ferrara, for it was here that the Este family established one of the most brilliant courts of the Renaissance. It was also an Este who created the magnificent garden at Tivoli (page 287), and who laid out the grounds of Palazzo Quirinale in Rome (page 332).

The golden age of Ferrara ended in 1598. The heir presumptive, Cesare d'Este, was the natural son of his father. Clement VIII, seeing his opportunity, issued a hasty law disallowing inheritance by illegitimate children. Papal forces then evicted the Este, and the city was left to decay under a remote Vatican administration.

The quiet region of Le Marche lies on the eastern slopes of the Apennines and is mainly devoted to farming: the winters can be extremely harsh. The Apennine barrier meant that its cultural influences were Venetian rather than Roman.

The remarkable survival of the gardens in Le Marche is often attributed to the 'conservative nature' of its inhabitants. Whether one chooses to accept this generalisation, it is credible that this remote Adriatic region should have been isolated from the changing fashions that wreaked havoc in the gardens of northern and central Italy. As a result, the region represents a treat for garden travellers. The *giochi d'acqua* and water-powered automata of the villas Buonaccorsi and Caprile act as a key to understanding eighteenth-century humour.

NEAREST MAJOR TOWN Ancona
MAIN FEATURES perfectly maintained eighteenth-century garden, automata
PRE-BOOKING yes
OWNER Società Agripicena
ADDRESS Via Giardino 9, Potenza Picena I-62018, Le Marche; tel.: +39 (0)733 880355
LOCATION Potenza Picena is c. 30 kilometres south of Ancona. Follow signs to the garden from the centre of Potenza Picena. On arrival it is signposted as Ristorante La Villa and Ristorante Il Fauno. On arrival go through the arch to the left of the bell, have patience and the gardener will admit you
OPEN March to September, Saturday, 8.00–12.00 by appointment only (preferably groups). It may be possible to visit during the week, by arrangement
ADMISSION fee on application
WHEELCHAIRS no
REFRESHMENTS two restaurants, booking advised
LAVATORIES yes

This wonderful garden, for many years designated a national monument, seems still to exist in the eighteenth century. The outside world has largely ignored it, few people have written about it, and its history is mostly unknown.

The villa was built in 1540 and a garden must have been laid out at the same time, though there is no record of it. It is possible that the remarkable stone-edged parterres on the upper terrace are relics from this period. The style made its appearance at the end of the fifteenth century, though examples of it are rare in Italy today. An eighteenth-century painting that used to belong to the family shows the garden almost exactly as it is now. While it is generally accepted that the garden was laid out afresh at this time, the style is really that of the previous century. Perhaps the alleged conservatism of Le Marche accounts for this.

emilia-romagna and le marche

The new wing and terrace were added on the occasion of the marriage of the late Count Buonaccorsi in 1910. His widow maintained the house and garden with loving care until her death in 1979. Fortunately for the future of the garden, its new owners intend to undertake a full programme of restoration.

The garden consists of five terraces descending from the villa. The upper three are almost exactly as they were during the eighteenth century, even down to the lemon trees espaliered along their walls. Considering that the lemons have to be covered against frost for several months each winter, this exemplifies the devotion with which the Buonaccorsi tended their garden over the centuries.

One enters the garden on the highest terrace that acts as the *giardino segreto*. It consists of four stone-edged parterres each divided into a variety of shapes such as stars, lozenges, and so on. The colourfully planted parterres contain potted lemons and eccentric little obelisks with ball feet. A pool in the centre of the terrace is surrounded by theatrically dressed putti, a number of Venetian figures complete the scene. The statues demonstrate how Le Marche looked north to Venice rather than to Rome or Florence for cultural inspiration.

The family chapel is at one end of the terrace. Almost hidden behind a huge clipped cypress hedge, it resembles a small man wearing an outsize false beard. At the opposite end of the terrace steps lead down to a small courtyard beside the villa. The garden wall here is decorated with mosaic and has a niche containing Pan. Continuing round the front of the villa one finds the aviary, decorated with tufa and occupied by canaries. A fountain plays inside it for their benefit.

Beneath the villa at the end of this path lies a grotto. Inside, a life-size monk is at prayer, while another looks in horror at the devil whose wooden head pops out from a hole in the rock as you enter. *Giochi d'acqua* in the ceiling would once have guaranteed a drenching.

The second terrace contains a number of simple parterres, with citrus trees espaliered against the retaining wall. Four elaborately carved obelisks stand along the central path.

The third terrace is narrower than the others. Known as the 'Viale degli Imperatori' from the imperial busts that line it, it is in effect a simple gravel walk where one can stroll without the risk of being mocked by the grotesque dwarves and *commedia dell'arte* figures who populate the other terraces. At one end stands a nymphaeum occupied by Flora, the presiding deity of the garden, who is crowned with a star whose points once sprayed water. From the nymphaeum a *berceau* runs back up to the chapel. It is densely covered in a wonderful tangle of ivy, jasmine and Russian vine.

The fourth and fifth terraces were probably planted at a slightly later date than the others. The fourth contains simple rectangular parterres that are a mass of colour during the summer. The retaining wall is set with wall fountains and is covered with valerian and climbing rose. Stone benches are arranged here for the view back at the garden above.

The lowest level consists of a series of private shaded walks between high laurel hedges and deep lily pools alive with frogs. In the centre of the high boundary wall that ends this terrace is one of the garden's many extraordinary survivals. This is the collection of water-powered automata that stand in a small shell-covered grotto. In the centre a life-size wooden huntsman sits on a rock, his hunting-horn at his lips. Behind him in niches are a Turk, a harlequin and a little group of smiths around their forge. Their mechanisms are still intact, and they are even clothed in faded and tattered eighteenth-century costumes. The automata are almost the only surviving examples of their kind and will be fully restored by the owners.

Farther along the wall is the capacious *limonaia*, with its built-in stoves as a necessary precaution against the cold Marche winters. Immediately beyond is the nineteenth-century *bosco* carefully land-scaped in the Romantic manner; on a hot day it is pleasant to wander among the full-grown ilexes and the Venetian statues. There is a series of pools and cascades (currently dry) and at one point the path spirals up a mount, though the view from the top is obscured by trees. Eventually the path leads back to the garden just below the chapel.

NEAREST MAJOR TOWN Pesaro
MAIN FEATURES eighteenth-century
garden, many working *giochi d'acqua*
PRE-BOOKING no
OWNER Instituto Tecnico Agrario
Statale 'A Cecchi'
ADDRESS Via Caprile 1, I-61100 Pesaro,
Le Marche;
tel.: +39 (0)721 21418/21440
LOCATION From the centre of Pesaro

follow signs to Rimini on the ss16. On
the outskirts of the town, the Institute
is signposted to the right.
OPEN 1 July to 15 September,
15.00–19.00
ADMISSION L5000, children L1000
WHEELCHAIRS no
REFRESHMENTS no
LAVATORIES yes

Since the fifteenth century the wealthy families of Pesaro have built summer residences on the slopes of the Colle San Bartolo above the city, following the lead of the Sforza at Villa Imperiale (page 254). Villa Caprile started life as a hunting lodge of the local Mosca family. In 1640 Marchese Giovanni Mosca began to turn it into a more substantial building. In 1763 Francesco Mosca had the villa considerably enlarged by Carlo Marchionni, and over the next 20 years the gardens took their present form. The green theatre, with seats clipped from cypress, was constructed at this time, though little remains of it today.

From 1817 to 1818 the villa was occupied by Princess Caroline of Brunswick and her paramour Bartolomeo Pergami. In 1876 it was acquired by a school of agriculture, and in 1934 became a State Agricultural Institute. During the Second World War the villa was used as a strongpoint on the Gothic Line, and was badly damaged as a consequence. The occupying German Army also felled the cypress avenue to give a clear field of fire. It was replanted immediately after the war, but sadly the trees are now diseased and are again being felled and replaced. A general programme of restoration is underway with assistance from the provincial administration of Pesaro.

The garden of Villa Caprile consists of three descending terraces directly in front of the villa. The highest terrace, protected on three sides by its retaining walls from the bitter Marche winds, is planted with parterres in box and myrtle. These are filled with annuals. This is not traditional but is done, as a staff member told us, to please visitors. As far as is possible the Institute grows the plants traditional to this garden; plumbago, bougainvillaea and old rose among others. They are aided by the extremely sheltered nature of the garden and by the huge underground spring-fed reservoirs dug when the house was first rebuilt. However, climate change has meant the loss of a number of species, among them acacia and a century-old *Kolreuteria paniculata* more than 9 metres high.

Beneath the steps leading down to this terrace lie several grottoes. The central one, flanked by dolphins whose eyes spurt water, is decorated with mosaic and *spugne*. Visible through a hole in the rock are little figures rotating solemnly. Water can spray out from a star in front and also from the metal flower in the ceiling. Immediately to the right is the '*grotta dell' orologio*' where water sprays from the clock inside. To the left of the central grotto lies yet another, occupied by a labyrinth of pipework and carefully labelled stopcocks. Here the controller of the *giochi d'acqua* stands, able to watch his guests' reactions through a peephole to the next grotto. The entire length of the retaining wall has been fitted with pipework and sprays, so there is no position of safety. Even the forewarned, leaning over the balustrade to watch their friends' discomfort, could be soaked by water jetting upward from the balustrade itself!

Further along the wall to the right is the most beautifully decorated of all the grottoes. Two small alabaster busts guard the entrance. The floor inside is mosaic, while walls and ceiling are of *spugne* inset with shells in a delicate pattern. Razor shells have also been used, whose mother-of-pearl surfaces give a lustrous glow to the interior. Even in this setting, however, one is not safe from the robust humour of the garden designer. A wooden hatch flies open to reveal the devil, complete with pitchfork. One is invited to touch him for luck. Needless to say on doing so water jets from his mouth, and for good measure from floor and ceiling as well. In the centre of the terrace the fountain was once in the form of a great metal globe. It is now thickly covered with moss and fern that gives it a strangely beautiful effect.

There are two seats at the head of the steps leading to the next terrace. Should a visitor pick the wrong one, they will be clamped to the seat while jets of water strike them in the face.

The lower terraces were undergoing substantial restoration on our visit, and it was not possible to see them. However, they contain two large fountains, one of Atlas bearing the world on his back. The other has a metal ball bobbing on a jet of water above an iron basket. The lowest terrace was the original fruit and vegetable garden, though it is now planted with scented shrubs.

emilia-romagna and le marche

villa imperiale

NEAREST MAJOR TOWN Pesaro
MAIN FEATURES unique sixteenth-century hanging garden
PRE-BOOKING organised tours only
OWNER Conte Guglielmo Castelbarco
ADDRESS Via S Bartolo 63, I-61100 Pesaro, Le Marche; tel.: +39 (0)721 23603

OPEN June to September, guided tours only. Apply to Azienda di Soggiorno di Pesaro, Piazza della Libertà, tel.: +39 (0)721 69341
ADMISSION L8000 (includes transport)
WHEELCHAIRS no
REFRESHMENTS no
LAVATORIES yes

The earliest house on this site, which still exists and forms part of the present complex of buildings, was erected by the Sforza family during the first half of the fifteenth century. The villa received its name after the visit in 1452 of Emperor Frederick III to Alessandro Sforza, then Governor of Pesaro. By the 1520s the house was owned by Francesco Maria Della Rovere, Duke of Urbino, and his wife Leonora Gonzaga. In 1522 they began a huge programme of reconstruction. Rome was by now the leader in architectural design, and the ducal architect Girolamo Gengo is known to have been influenced by Raphael. Georgina Masson describes the duke giving Gengo one of Raphael's letters in which his ideas are set out for Villa Madama in Rome (page 320).

Following the complete redecoration of the old house, the new villa was constructed and gardens laid out on the hillside above the site. The resulting building was for many years one of the most famous in Italy.

During the seventeenth century the Della Rovere line died out and the villa passed by marriage to a branch of the Medici family. It was no longer occupied and fell into decay. Severe damage sustained during the Second World War might have seen the end of it, had it not been for the dedicated attention of its present owner.

From a distance it is the old fifteenth-century building with its tall watchtower that predominates. As one approaches the ingenuity of the construction becomes apparent. Connected to the earlier building by a bridge, the newer villa lies between it and the steeply rising ground beyond. At either end it extends narrow wings into the hillside on which the garden is laid out. The result is that there is a central court-yard enclosed on three sides by the villa and overlooked on the fourth side by terraces. As well as the intended design for Villa Madama this also recalls Donato Bramante's plans for the Cortile del Belvedere in the Vatican, begun c. 1505 (page 337).

From the villa a shady portico opens into the courtyard. This is now laid out with eight rectangular beds, bordered with pebbles and planted with annuals. All around are walls set with scores of niches containing terracotta urns and amphorae whose colour harmonises perfectly with the pale brick. Spiral staircases and passages in each of the wings to left and right lead to the first terrace which contains the *limonaia* and several simple parterres. Its walls are densely covered with wisteria. One would think that this terrace alone would be enough work for the single gardener employed.

The stairs lead to one of a pair of loggias in front of the upper gar-den. The topiary this once held has long since vanished, and the pre-sent owner has replanted it as a parterre garden, ornamented with potted lemon trees. The walls are still covered with espaliered fruit trees as they were originally. The semicircular loggias in the corners, which gave access to the surrounding *bosco*, have disappeared.

Returning to the front of the terrace, a balustraded walk runs along the top of each connecting wing to two more loggias at each end of the villa. The view from these is superb.

NEAREST MAJOR TOWN Ferrara

MAIN FEATURES early sixteenth-century parterre garden, maze

PRE-BOOKING no

OWNER the State

ADDRESS Via xx Settembre 124, Ferrara

LOCATION the palazzo is in the south-east corner of the city not far from the Porta Romana

OPEN all year 9.00–16.00, closed Monday and national holidays

ADMISSION free (garden only)

WHEELCHAIRS yes

REFRESHMENTS no

LAVATORIES yes

Palazzo di Ludovico il Moro was built between 1495 and 1503. The project was commissioned by Antonio Costabili, Ferrarese Ambassador to the Milanese court. The Duke of Milan at that time was Ludovico Sforza, il Moro (the Moor), which is presumably why the palazzo incorrectly bears his name. It has been said that Ludovico had it built as a bolt-hole after the invasion of Charles VIII of France. This is plausible, especially as Ludovico's wife, Beatrice, was the daughter of Ercole d'Este, but the documentary evidence does not support it.

The palazzo was designed by Biagio Rossetti, the principal Ferrarese architect under Ercole I. Since 1492 he had been working on the 'Addizione Erculea', the carefully planned expansion to the north of the city. In addition, he was responsible for the building of no less than eight palaces and four churches in the city. This enormous amount of work perhaps explains why the palazzo was never completed (two sides of the courtyard remain unfinished).

The palazzo left the ownership of the Costabili with the passing of Este rule, and has changed hands many times over the centuries. In 1920 it was acquired by the State in a ruinous condition, and was restored in the 1930s. It currently houses the Archaeological Museum.

emilia-romagna and le marche

The roughly square garden is on the far side of Rossetti's uncompleted courtyard. The palazzo forms one side and part of another, while the remainder is walled. As one stands under the arcade, a row of four large, rounded cones of yew, whose shapes echo the graceful curve of the arches above, can be seen.

The original design of the garden is not known. However, as it stands it is purely Renaissance in style, and it can be safely assumed that the earliest garden would have been similar. The designer has made maximum use of the limited space available by repeatedly dividing and subdividing the area with hedges of yew and box, separated by narrow gravel paths. There is a maze in the centre of the garden, but the overall effect is of one enormous labyrinth.

The garden is divided roughly into three by two shady avenues running the length of it. One is of pollarded limes; the other is a dense tunnel of roses. At an intersection in the rose tunnel is the well that has a fine Venetian well-head carved with acanthus leaves, and ornate wrought-iron decoration on the support for the pulley. At the far end of this most peaceful of urban gardens, filled with the sound of wood pigeons, rises a screen of tall cypresses.

lazio

regional introduction

The history of Lazio (Latium) is effectively the history of Rome. In turn, the period of interest is largely dominated by the deeds of the Papacy. It was not till 1417 that the Papacy was firmly re-established in Rome after the turbulent events of the thirteenth and fourteenth centuries. During the following years the influence of the Tuscan Renaissance began to be felt. By the end of the century Roman artists and architects had devised their own distinctive style. Both spiritual and temporal rulers made full use of it.

The importance of the Roman Renaissance in garden design lies in its recognition that a garden could create a specific visual effect by the use of perspective, changes of level and an axial layout. From being a place of retreat where man drew consolation from nature, the garden became a place for display where nature was at the service of man. This understanding of the malleability of landscape lies at the heart of all subsequent garden design.

NEAREST MAJOR TOWN Rome
MAIN FEATURES early baroque garden
on a steep site, large water theatre,
water staircase
PRE-BOOKING no
OWNER Principe Aldobrandini
ADDRESS Via G Massaia 18, I-00044
Frascati
LOCATION Frascati is 20 kilometres
south-east of Rome on the SS215.
Enter the main piazza, with the villa
visible above it, and Via G Massaia is
in the far-left corner
OPEN Monday to Friday 9.00–13.00
(garden only); entrance passes only
available from APT, Piazza Marconi 1,
I-00044 Frascati; tel. +39 (0)6
9420331
ADMISSION free
WHEELCHAIRS yes, as far as the water
theatre
REFRESHMENTS no
LAVATORIES no

Villa Aldobrandini was built between 1598 and 1603 for Cardinal Pietro Aldobrandini. He came from a Tuscan family that achieved prominence when Ippolito Aldobrandini was elected to the Papacy as Clement VIII in 1592. His first act was to bestow a Cardinal's hat on his nephew Pietro.

In 1598 Pietro acted as his uncle's strong-arm man in the eviction of the Este from their city of Ferrara. As a reward for this Clement bestowed on him not only the revenues of the Duchy of Ferrara, but also an estate above Frascati seized the previous year. A simple villa already stood on the site: it had been erected in the 1560s by Pier Antonio Contugi, doctor to Pius IV. The cardinal commissioned Giacomo della Porta to design the new villa, which incorporated much of the earlier building. Della Porta's died in 1602 and the villa was completed the following year by Carlo Maderno with the assistance of Giovanni Fontana. In 1603 the cardinal persuaded a neighbour to allow

him water rights over his land, and built around 13 kilometres of aqueduct and canal to bring water to his garden. The great waterworks it was to supply were designed by Orazio Olivieri who had been curator of the fountains at the Villa d'Este (page 287). Aldobrandini was particularly anxious that his villa should surpass that of Cardinal Gambara at Villa Lante, Bagnaia (page 314) who is said to have paid

70,000 *scudi* on the waterworks there – a very inferior sum to that paid by his rival.

Pietro found little favour with his uncle's successor, the Borghese Paul v. His Ferrarese revenues were stopped and in 1610 he was placed under house arrest. He died without an heir in 1621 and the property passed to his cousins. However, a trust had been established to preserve the family name. Ironically, it was a Borghese who assumed the title of Prince Aldobrandini during the last century.

The villa and gardens were badly damaged by Allied bombing during the Anzio landings in 1943. They have since been restored by the owners, but much of the garden is sadly run down at present.

This enormous villa towers above the little town of Frascati. Originally approached from the entrance in the middle of the town, it must have grown ever more impressive when approached up the ilex-shaded central avenue. To either side stretched a broad *tapis vert*, with two further avenues running diagonally to each end of the villa.

Now, however, the gates are rusted shut, as they have for more than a century; also the ilexes now form an impassable tunnel and the *tapis vert* is no more than rough pasture. The present entrance is from the steep lane to the left that leads to the great oval terrace below the villa. From here ramps lead to an upper terrace and down to join the original entrance avenue. Two grottoes are placed on the central axis: one at the head of the avenue, the other at the back of the oval terrace. From the upper terrace a door in the wall to the left of the villa leads to a grove, more correctly perhaps a quincunx, of ancient pollarded planes whose huge, grotesque forms are straight out of Rackham. Originally a large parterre garden lay beyond this, but it no longer exists. The pattern is repeated at the other end of the villa, where the parterres still survive, and the plane grove is filled with large hydrangeas. Beyond the plane trees a path leads to a small *broderie* garden planted in the shape of the family crest.

Between the groves, opposite the villa, is the garden's famous water theatre. Several authors have found the feature disproportionately large for the narrow space behind the villa, though it is undeniably

impressive. In the centre stands Atlas (sculpted by Jaques Saracin in 1620) with water pouring over him as he struggles to support the globe. At his feet the buried Titan Enceladus struggles for freedom. (It is said that he is imprisoned beneath Sicily, hence its frequent earthquakes.) Other scholars have identified the titan as Tantalus, who symbolises the fate of those that reject divine wisdom. According to an illustration by G B Falda of the seventeenth century, Atlas was once aided by Hercules. This would have been a dual allusion: first to the legend of the Hesperides, to which reference is made in the other decorations of the theatre, and second to Pietro's assistance to Clement in the matter of Ferrara, which is also mentioned in the inscription around the top of the theatre. However, Falda's work is not always reliable: his curious identification of Pan, on the left of the theatre, as the one-eyed Polyphemus is a case in point. In a niche on the other side is a horn-playing centaur. This, and Pan, are relics of an extraordinary orchestra that played a variety of water-powered instruments under the direction of Apollo. The reliefs, busts and statues were originally polychrome and were all the work of Ippolito Buti. The other figures have now vanished. Their disappearance would have pleased President de Brosses who, after a visit to the villa in 1740, commented: 'What can be more chilling than to see these stone creatures, daubed with colour, making melancholy music without piping or moving?' He may, of course, have been disgruntled after being soaked through twice in a day by *giochi d'acqua*.

The two chambers to left and right are respectively a chapel dedicated to St Sebastian, and the 'Room of the Winds'. The latter continued the theme hinted at by the 'orchestra' with a representation of Mount Parnassus, home of the Muses, and a statue of Pegasus. The seventeenth-century English diarist and garden writer John Evelyn famously described a 'copper ball that continually dances about three foot above the pavement by virtue of a winde conveyed secretly to a hole beneath it'.

The broad stone terrace above the theatre is reached by a sloping ramp. From here there is a fine view of the villa, with the Apennines lining the horizon. Immediately above the theatre the line of the central axis continues with a steep water staircase. At its head it is flanked by two tall columns whose summits shoot jets of water that then fall in the runnels which spiral down the sides like helter-skelters.

There are two further cascades above this point. Although the steps are dangerous and the climb steep, it is worth making the climb for it is here that the major differences between this garden and its predecessors are best appreciated. First, the villa is intended as the centrepiece of the garden and so blocks the view that in an earlier garden would have been left open. Second, the boundaries of the garden change rapidly from an artificial to a rural landscape. This was originally symbolised by the highest cascade, known as the Fountain of the Shepherds (and which was mostly destroyed during the war). Simple rides trail off into the *bosco* that presses closely in on either side.

NEAREST MAJOR TOWN Viterbo

MAIN FEATURES woodland walks, grotto in the cliffs

PRE-BOOKING yes, by appointment with Signora Maria Pace Guidotto, or with the shipping lines (see below)

OWNER Family del Drago

ADDRESS Isola Bisentina, Lago di Bolsena, I-01010 Capodimonte; tel.: +39 (0)761 799820

LOCATION the island can be reached by boat, either from Capodimonte (Navigazione la Bussola; tel.: +39 (0)761 870760) or from Bolsena (Navigazione Alto Lazio; tel.: +39(0)761 798033 or (0)336 764179)

OPEN 1 April to 1 October

ADMISSION L10,000 for a guided tour

WHEELCHAIRS no

REFRESHMENTS no

LAVATORIES yes

The island's earliest inhabitants were Etruscan who were later succeeded by the Romans. During the Middle Ages a feud between the lords of the surrounding region resulted in the medieval settlement being burnt to the ground. In 1261, Urban IV had an ecclesiastical prison built on the island for the incarceration of heretics.

By the fifteenth century the island was inhabited by an order of monks. It belonged to the powerful Farnese family, rulers of most of Tusculum. Rannuccio Farnese, who entered papal service as a diplomat, favoured the island monks and chose to be buried in their chapel. Isaia da Pisa was commissioned by him to design a tomb.

During the sixteenth century the island was a place of retreat for the Farnese popes. Papal apartments were built in the walls of the humble monastery and in 1516 Cardinal Alessandro Farnese, the future Paul III, commissioned Antonio di Sangallo the younger to design a cloister. In 1588, Giacomo Vignola designed the church of San Giovanni Battista and the three votive chapels on the southern side of the

island. It was during this period that walks were made through the ilex woods and a cool grotto was cut from the tufa cliff at the water level.

Throughout the Renaissance the island continued to serve a dual purpose. With its votive chapels linked by beautiful paths through the woods and along the cliffs, it was an ideal place of penitence and retreat. In complete contrast it was also used by the Farnese as a *barco* or hunting wood. The island is currently owned by Principe Giovanni del Drago, who is restoring the buildings and recreating gardens beneath the walls of San Giovanni.

boat house, along the water's edge, while beneath its towering walls
the present owner has planted a charming Italianate garden. The layout was inspired by Giusto Utens' lunette of the Medici garden at
Petraia (page 199). Enclosed by a young box hedge, the beds are
packed to overflowing with sweet-scented annuals, while the palms,
horse chestnuts, limes and magnificent magnolia create a towering
backdrop to this part of the garden.

The beautiful nave of the church has the celebrated Farnese
(c. 1440) tomb by Isaia da Pisa. During the summer, the church is
the setting for classical concerts. The doorway frames a magnificent
view through the trees to the water's edge.

Beyond the church, Sangallo's cloister has been beautifully restored
by the owner. Pots of trailing geranium stand on the walls and around
the ornate nymphaeum. A rose pergola links the end of the cloister to
the gate. The land to the south of the church is enclosed by stone walls.
Once the walled orchard of the monastery, the area is now maintained
as rough pasture. Beyond, the grass gives way to a dense ilex wood
where the Farnese had paths cut through the undergrowth – which
consists largely of bay and myrtle. The penitential walk between the
seven votive chapels follows a most beautiful route from the depths of
the woods to the cliff's edge.

Traces of Paul III's Giardino delle Delizie are all over the island.
At its southernmost end an artificial grotto has been carved out of the
soft tufa at water level. Elsewhere, ferocious stone lions emerge from
the undergrowth.

NEAREST MAJOR TOWN Viterbo

MAIN FEATURES sixteenth-century mannerist fantasy garden in a woodland setting

PRE-BOOKING no

OWNER Signore Giovanni Bettini

ADDRESS I-01020 Bomarzo

LOCATION well signposted (Parco dei Mostri) from the centre of town

OPEN 8.30–dusk

ADMISSION L12,000, children aged 3–8 years L8000, reductions for groups and students

WHEELCHAIRS no

REFRESHMENTS yes

LAVATORIES yes

Sacro Bosco, or 'sacred grove', was built by Pier Francesco 'Vicino' Orsini. It has been attributed to many artists over the years, but it is likely that Orsini planned the park, hiring sculptors and a team of labourers to bring his ideas into being. Work began in 1552 but as a soldier in Paul III's army Orsini was away from home almost continually till 1567. He fought in Germany, Flanders and the Papal States, and spent a couple of years as a prisoner of war. It was only when he retired at the age of 54 that Orsini could devote himself entirely to the park and he continued to work on Sacro Bosco till his death in 1584.

Orsini was not a powerful man in a political sense but was an important figure in the intellectual world, and he moved freely among the educated men of his day. As the husband of Giulia Farnese he became an *habitué* of her cousin's palace in Caprarola (page 303). Cardinal Gambara of Villa Lante (page 314) also was his friend and Sacro Bosco gave expression to all these aspects of his life. In it he made three-dimensional his love and knowledge of literature and his personal philosophy. He also mocked the pomposities of his more illustrious friends.

lazio

Although the park was famous during Orsini's lifetime, when he died it fell almost at once into obscurity. It seems that it was never visited by any of the great travellers and diarists of the seventeenth and eighteenth centuries, perhaps because it was shunned by the locals. In 1645 the property was sold to the della Rovere family, and in 1845 it was sold again to the Borghese who bought it as part of agricultural land. The fortunes of Sacro Bosco changed dramatically in 1949 when it was visited by the Spanish surrealist Salvador Dalí who found the place in ruins as a result of earthquakes. The large statues were completely overgrown, and the smaller ones were strewn about the woods. Dalí's visit brought the park back into the public eye and three years later the University of Rome undertook the massive job of piecing together the original layout and seeking out the archival material to help their task. In 1954 Signor Giovanni Bettini bought the site and together with his late wife devoted himself to its restoration.

Sacro Bosco is best seen on a winter's day in mid-week. When it is deserted, and the statues stand abandoned among the fallen leaves, it is possible to catch something of the mysterious atmosphere that Orsini wished to create. He lived at a time when it was becoming fashionable to convert the family stronghold into a Renaissance villa and to lay out gardens in place of the fortifications. Orsini's palace is still perched on a cliff high above the park. He bowed to fashion to the extent of creating a small terraced garden below it. However, his real enthusiasm was reserved for the rocky slope 400 metres away. He planted trees to create his sacred grove, and then had a phantasmagoria of statues and monuments hewn from lumps of tufa that lay scattered on the site and painted in bright colours. When it was complete, the park could just be seen from the north-facing apartments of the palace.

Such was the power of the local legends that grew up around Orsini's monsters that in 1980 an altar was erected in the park and an official exorcism performed. However, it seems unlikely that Orsini intended to frighten his visitors: they could have 'read' his creation rather as they would a book. His theme was man's journey through the snares and passions of the world to an understanding of divine love. Broadly speaking, this idea had been explored by both Petrarch and Dante Alghieri, poets of the Middle Ages who had laid the foundations for the literature of the Renaissance. It was a theme that Orsini could explore in relation to his own life, thereby creating in the park a kind of personal monument. He chose to base many of the statues on the extraordinary figures that people the pages of Ariosto's epic poem *Orlando Furioso* (composed between 1506 and 1532). (For an exhaustive account of the iconography, see the article by Margaretta J Darnall and Mark S Weil in the bibliography.)

Orsini's voice is audible in every corner of the park in the form of the inscriptions picked out in red paint on the lichen-covered stone. Many inscriptions acted as keys to an interpretation of the place and could be traced back to Dante, Petrarch and Ariosto. Others were the words of Orsini who, like a good storyteller, constantly reminded his visitors of the extraordinary nature of what they were seeing. The park was laid out on three levels, with the Temple of Divine Love at the top. Visitors originally entered by way of a small bridge over the stream at the bottom and the first things they saw were the towering figures of the two struggling giants. As one giant was tearing the other apart by the legs, the visitors would have been witnessing a scene from *Orlando Furioso* where in his madness Orlando rent a woodcutter in two.

Entering by way of a new bridge further up-stream, one passes the

end of an avenue of fountains leading to a huge, open-mouthed mask. The mask marks the point where the stream enters the garden and it is surmounted by the globe and castle of the Orsini family crest, which are cut out of the rock.

Continuing past the giants to the lowest level of the garden one is greeted by an extraordinary sight. A huge, moss-covered tortoise supports a statue of Fame blowing a trumpet. Contemporary visitors would have recognised the group as a reference to the old aphorism *festina lente*, or 'make haste slowly', which in visual terms was formed by the combination of almost anything with a tortoise.

Beyond the tortoise a statue of Pegasus on a rock rises out of the tilting bowl of a fountain which once poured water into the stream below. Pegasus was a familiar symbol among the rich and the great. From his hoof mark on Mount Helicon the spring of the Muses flowed into their gardens. The Villa d'Este at Tivoli (page 287) exemplifies Pegasus' role in drawing attention to the owner's prowess as an intellectual and a patron of the arts. By placing the fountain at the lowest level of the garden, in absurd juxtaposition to the tortoise, Orsini succeeded in mocking the pomposity of Ippolito d'Este and others like him.

Continuing on the same level, one arrives in a shady grove. The stone seats on either side of the path are large enough to accommodate two people – they are lovers' seats. A bas-relief set in the hillside on the left shows The Three Graces, with their bottoms in high relief. Beyond them are the remains of a nymphaeum that was once enclosed and which contained a fountain surrounded by cupids. This area represents an earthly paradise, from which the visitor must free himself to follow the higher calling of divine love.

A clearing beyond the grove is the site of a theatre, formed by a curving wall set against the slope. The niches once held statues, and the top of the wall was decorated with a balustrade. The remains of the balustrade can be seen in the undergrowth below the clearing, near the bowl of an unfinished fountain.

At one end of the clearing Orsini built a dramatically leaning house. The simple building's only decoration is a bear, or *orso*, holding the Orsini arms and shield. It is said that the house was built to reveal the corrupt nature of the world: when one stands on its sloping floor all the monuments outside appear to tilt.

A long terrace lies above the clearing, on the second of the park's three levels. It is lined with enormous urns that are not unlike Etruscan funerary vases. This level is peopled with a selection of extraordinary figures, each imbued with its own significance. At one end is a colossal female figure with a vase on her head. She is sometimes said to represent lasciviousness on account of her voluptuousness and the image of two harpies torturing a man carved on her broad back.

The shallow pool at the end of the terrace is guarded by a river god, not dissimilar to those at Villa Lante (page 314). The colossal female figure to his left may represent Angelica, the object of Orlando's unrequited passion. A dog stands guard over her recumbent form.

To the right of the fountain is a griffin locked in mortal combat with two lions. No one has managed to fit the elephant that stands below them into a credible iconographic account of the park. Clad in the full regalia of war, it squeezes the life out of a Roman soldier with its trunk.

The Hell Mouth, perhaps the most famous of the monuments, is also on this level. It forms part of a monstrous face, with flared nostrils and staring eyes. A flight of steps leads into the mouth where a stone bench and table seem to suggest that it would be a good place for a picnic. The structure was built to amplify and distort sound, and it is said that the voices of anyone inside can be heard all over the park.

On the third and highest level Orsini built his own version of the hippodrome that had recently been excavated at Hadrian's Villa (page 287). Giant acorns and pine-cones decorate the edges, while the oaks that stand to one side of it shower real acorns in the autumn. The area is guarded by fish-tailed harpies, lions and bear cubs which hold the Orsini arms and rosette. The three-headed dog of the underworld, Cerberus, sits under a nut tree at one end.

The Temple of Divine Love stands on a slope above the hippodrome and represents the ultimate goal for travellers through the garden. Its simple structure is decorated with the Orsini rosettes and Farnese lilies. The door mouldings are made from parts of Etruscan tombs found on site. Orsini dedicated the temple to his wife on her death, and the present owner has followed his example.

NEAREST MAJOR TOWN Rome
MAIN FEATURES seventeenth-century villa and museum, large landscaped park
PRE-BOOKING no
OWNER the State
ADDRESS Piazzale Flaminio, I-00196 Rome
LOCATION Villa Borghese is in the park

of the same name in central Rome
METRO Flaminio
TRAM 19, 30
BUS 202, 203, 205, 490, 495
OPEN dawn to dusk
ADMISSION free
WHEELCHAIRS yes
REFRESHMENTS yes
LAVATORIES yes

In 1605 Cardinal Scipione Borghese began to buy land on the Pincian Hill just north of Rome's city walls. Born Scipione Caffarelli, he had been made a cardinal by his uncle Paul V on condition that he took the family name. A gentle and generous man, known as the 'delight of Rome', he was also a collector of considerable wealth and taste. The villa, or casino, was never meant to be lived in. It was designed instead as a gallery for his collection, much of which is still in situ. Initially Flaminio Ponzio was commissioned as architect, but he died almost immediately. The work was taken over by Johann van Santen, an architect from Utrecht known in Italy as Giovanni Vansanzio. The casino was completed by 1616 and Girolamo Rainaldi lay the formal gardens around it between 1617 and 1619. It is likely that he was also responsible for the charmingly frivolous baroque aviary. Pietro Bernini created most of the garden sculpture.

Very little of the seventeenth-century garden survives. In c. 1789 the grounds were relaid by Jacob Moore, a Scottish painter resident in Rome who was a protégé of the Prince Borghese of the time. He laid out the hippodrome, the lake and possibly the Temple of Aesculapius,

though this can be dated to a later remodelling of the gardens in 1849.

Shortly after completion of the villa a plaque was erected at the main garden entrance. The Latin verses on it read, in part, as follows: 'I, custodian of Villa Borghese on the Pincio, proclaim the following: Whoever you are, if you are free, do not fear here the fetters of the law. Go where you wish, pluck what you wish, leave when you wish. These things are provided more for strangers than for the owner ...'. This was

not always heeded by the owners. A first attempt to close the park had failed in 1828. A later generation of Borghese, hoping to sell off most of the land to developers, were taken to court and defeated by the municipality of Rome in 1885. Rights of access were awarded on four afternoons a week. In 1902, the family, bankrupted by building speculation, was forced to sell the estate to the Republic for L3 million. Villa Borghese was the first of the great Roman parks intended for pub-

lazio

lic enjoyment, and it still serves that function. It is the 'green lung' of Rome, covering an enormous area and being densely wooded. It is this that makes it so pleasurable to wander in and explore.

The casino was built in a corner of the park. It had its own small formal gardens that still survive, though in poor condition. The secret gardens lie on either side of the casino, and there is a *broderie* parterre garden immediately behind it. The balustrade set with fountains that encloses the rear garden and the front courtyard is an early twentieth-century copy. The original was sold to Viscount Astor in 1896 and is splendidly relocated along the great terrace at Cliveden in Buckinghamshire. The garden and courtyard entrances are guarded by herms.

There is an aviary at the end of the narrow secret garden to the left of the casino. It is equipped with four wrought-iron domes that rise most oddly above the baroque pediments. The narrow strip of formal garden extends in a straight line into the park. On the far side of the aviary is a small dining pavilion. Beyond this the garden slopes gently downwards, overlooked by a balustraded terrace. Fruit trees are espaliered against the retaining wall.

Little else remains of the original layout. Rainaldi's open-air theatre survives to the north-west of the casino, and Bernini's herms look down on the old chestnut-sellers. The regular pattern of paths and groves with a fountain or statue at each intersection has been replaced by meandering paths and broad avenues. Moore's English garden covers the western end of the park, with its lake (where boats may be hired) and classical temple. It is nonetheless an enjoyable place to wander in, watching the entertaining procession passing on horseback, bicycle, roller-skate and, sometimes, on foot.

NEAREST MAJOR TOWN Rome
MAIN FEATURES sixteenth-century garden famous for its fountains
PRE-BOOKING no
OWNER the State
ADDRESS Piazza Trento 1, I-00019 Tivoli; tel.: +39 (0)774 22070
LOCATION Tivoli is east of Rome on the SS5 (Via Tiburtina); or take the A24 and the Tivoli exit (quicker). The villa is in the centre of town. Note that it is crowded on summer weekends and that parking can be difficult
OPEN Tuesday to Sunday, January, 9.00–16.00 (fountains 10.00–13.00, 14.00–16.30); February, 9.00–17.00 (14.00–17.30); March, 9.00–17.30 (14.00–19.00); April, 9.00–18.30 (14.00–19.30); May to August, 9.00–18.45 (14.00–19.30); September, 9.00–18.30 (14.00–19.30); October, 9.00–16.45 (14.00–17.30); November, 9.00–16.15 (14.00–17.30); December, 9.00–16.00 (14.00–16.00); exit 45 minutes after closing time
ADMISSION L8000, free to children under 18 years
WHEELCHAIRS no
REFRESHMENTS yes
LAVATORIES yes

The Villa d'Este was built c. 1555 by Pirro Ligorio for Cardinal Ippolito d'Este. Ippolito was the younger son of Alfonso I of Ferrara and his wife Lucrezia Borgia. A man of enormous ability and great wealth, Ippolito was not only a generous patron of all the arts, but also a knowledgeable and sensitive collector and antiquarian. It is said that it was his notorious ambition that finally denied him the papacy. When Julius III was elected in his place on a split vote he offered Ippolito the governorship of Tivoli in gratitude.

The governor's residence at Tivoli was the old Franciscan monastery and on his arrival in 1550 Ippolito immediately began its transformation. He commissioned Ligorio, who was at that time his Director of

Antiquities responsible for the excavation of the nearby Villa Adriana (Hadrian's Villa). Work on the gardens began in 1560 and was completed by 1575.

Ippolito died in 1572 and he left the property to any future cardinals in the family; should there be no suitable heir the villa was to go to the Dean of the College of Cardinals. His nephew Cardinal Luigi d'Este inherited the estate, but when he died in 1586 there was no Este cardinal and the property went to the dean, Alessandro Farnese, an old Este rival. Before he could take possession the Este stripped the villa and garden of everything moveable. When in 1605 the villa was returned to Cardinal Alessandro d'Este, the garden statuary was replaced, but by then Ligorio's subtle iconographical design had been hopelessly confused.

The decay of the gardens began in the eighteenth century. In 1787, the villa fell into Austrian hands by the marriage of Beatrice, last of the Este, to the Habsburg family. Like so many Habsburg properties in Italy, it was then completely neglected.

After the First World War the villa became the property of the Italian Republic and the gardens restored. During the Second World War the villa and gardens were heavily damaged by bombing, but have since been restored. The number and complexity of the waterworks means that constant maintenance has to be carried out. The planting, however, has been allowed to become much thicker than it would once have been. The gardens are so popular in summer that barriers channel visitors around the fountains; it is advised to go early or late in the year, and to avoid weekends.

Once coaches would arrive in Tivoli and leave their passengers at the bottom of the garden to make their own way up to the house.

Unfortunately, today the entrance is through the villa and it is advised that one goes straight down through the garden, looking neither right nor left, until the little gate at the far end of the central axis. On turning round, the garden will been seen (more or less) as the designer intended, with the steeply forested slope ascending to the villa. The basic plan of the garden is simple: a central axis with the two principal cross-axes running across it at right-angles.

It is important to understand that the whole garden was designed to glorify the cardinal not only just by its magnificence, but also by the use of a symbolism easily comprehensible to any educated person of the sixteenth century.

The passage is thought to have been covered by a pergola and was designed in the form of a cross centred on the cypress 'rotunda' in front, where some pictures record a grand octagonal pavilion. This no longer exists (if it ever did) and the rotunda has been restored to its seventeenth-century condition. It frames a view of the villa.

On the wall to the right is the fountain of the many-breasted Diana (Artemis) of Ephesus. A copy of a classical original in the Farnese collection, she was considered in the sixteenth century to represent Mother Nature. (She was also the divinity who gave St Paul so much trouble during his mission to the Ephesians.)

This is the flattest part of the garden and has simple square parterres. Originally it was planted with fruit trees and herbs. The two curious little hillocks on the right are called the *metae sudantes* and are miniature versions of the Meta Sudans, a huge fountain built by Domitian in AD 96 near the Colosseum in Rome. They were intended to be placed in the central fishpools; thankfully this was never done.

The three great rectangular fishpools form the first main cross-axis

of the garden. Their still waters reflect the roaring turbulence of the Fountain of Neptune at the far end, which was a simple cascade until 1927 when it was transformed by the addition of powerful jets. A continual rainbow hangs in the spray that surrounds it.

Above this great cataract stands the Organ Fountain. Constructed in 1568, it originally held the statue of Diana and was known as the Fountain of Nature. The organ itself was based on classical designs described by Vitruvius in the first century BC. Water pressure made it produce musical notes and even trumpet-calls automatically. The baroque portico behind it dates from 1611.

The ascent from the first cross-axis rises steeply towards the villa by means of three parallel staircases. The central stair is flanked by a descending water 'chain'. To its right is the stair of the 'Bollori' (boiling water). The steps are flanked by masks, all different, that spout water into basins where it is ingeniously made to froth and bubble.

The central stair ascends to the Fountain of the Dragon, where it divides and climbs in two beautiful curves around the fountain to the terrace above. The fountain represents the many-headed dragon Ladon who guarded the entrance to the Gardens of the Hesperides. A huge statue of Hercules, who vanquished Ladon, once stood in the niche behind the fountain. From the curving inner balustrades water was meant to spurt high into the air before dropping back into the pool beneath, while down the outer balustrades flowed streams of water gushing from the breasts of a pair of sphinxes on the terrace above.

This terrace forms the second main cross-axis. Known as the Path of the Hundred Fountains, it is perhaps the best-known feature of the gardens. Three parallel channels run along it, one above the other. The highest channel is fed by boat-shaped fountains and ornamented with fleur-de-lis, eagles and obelisks. Hundreds of little animal masks pour water from one level to the next. It was decorated with terracotta reliefs of Ovid's *Metamorphoses* (first century AD) but these have mostly disappeared, either decayed or concealed behind the dense mat of ferns that droop into the channels.

At the left-hand end of the path is the Oval Fountain in a shaded courtyard with stone tables and benches. A more beautiful place to dine on a summer's day is hard to imagine. The air is cooled by the great cascade that pours into a large oval pool, while nymphs on either side continually empty their urns into the water. A path that runs behind the pool has arches so that one may look out from behind the tumbling water. On top of an artificial mound above the cascade is a statue of Pegasus leaping into the air. There is also an empty grotto to one side of the courtyard that was once the Grotto of Venus.

At the opposite end of the path is the Fountain of the Rometta (Little Rome). A fountain shaped like a boat lies in front of a raised stage, in the centre of which is a statue representing Rome, with Romulus, Remus and the she-wolf to one side. To the left rises a curious collection of miniature buildings. These once extended all along the back of the stage and were intended as replicas of the monuments of classical Rome. Most of them, however, fell into the valley during the last century.

Below the Rometta lie two other fountains. One is dedicated to Proserpine and was originally known as the Fountain of the Emperors because it held statues of the four emperors known to have lived in the vicinity. The other, the Fountain of the Owl, once had a display of mechanical birds whose water-powered song continued until an owl appeared whose hooting frightened them into silence. It is now a simple fountain in a niche decorated with the Este eagle and fleur-de-lis, its columns beautifully entwined with mouldings of the Apples of the Hesperides.

At the very top of the garden, immediately below the retaining wall (which is densely covered with jasmine), is another transverse path, the Cardinal's Path, that runs from the Grotto of Aesculapius to the marvellous Grotto of Diana at the right-hand end. This is magnificently decorated with bas-reliefs of mythological acts of chastity; Diana and Actaeon, Perseus and Andromeda, Apollo and Daphne, and others. It once housed statues of Diana, Minerva and Hippolyta: they are now in the Capitoline Museum in Rome.

Finally, returning along the Cardinal's Path, the last steps to the central loggia can be climbed to enjoy the magnificent view over the valley. Beneath, the line of the central axis is completed by two last fountains, that of Pandora and, below her, Bernini's *Bicchierone*, or 'goblet'.

The garden symbolism mentioned above has been skilfully analysed by David R Coffin (see bibliography, page 379). There are three principal themes. The first concerns nature and art, and is developed along the two cross-axes. Thus on the lower axis life-giving waters stem from Mother Nature, fill the fishpools and irrigate fruits, vegetables and flowers. It was originally intended to build a fountain of the sea at the far end of the fishpools that was to contain a statue of Neptune and would have received all the waters of the garden. The upper axis, relating to art, begins where the hoof of Pegasus has struck out the spring sacred to the Muses. It flows to the Rometta, representative of man's greatest achievements.

The second theme also follows the upper axis. The Oval Fountain

is to be recognised as representing the real cascades of Tivoli. The three channels down which its water flows are the three local rivers that eventually join the Tiber at Rome, thus linking the locations of the cardinal's greatest achievements.

The final theme is the most important. This is based on the Este claim to be descended from Hercules, who is thus made the presiding deity of the garden. His statue, standing as it did midway between the grottoes of Venus and Diana, illustrated his legendary choice between vice and virtue. Having chosen the virtuous path he won the Apples of the Hesperides, emblematic of temperance and chastity, here repeatedly shown in the possession of the Este eagle. In this way the entire garden glorifies both the cardinal's virtues and his ability to transform nature into art.

NEAREST MAJOR TOWN Rome

MAIN FEATURES seventeenth-century *casino*, garden and park

PRE-BOOKING no

OWNER Comune di Roma

ADDRESS Via Aurelia Antica, 1-00165 Rome

LOCATION the entrance to the park is beyond Porta San Pancrazio. The casino is a 10-minute walk from a small, unattended car park at the junction of Via San Pancrazio and Via Aurelia Antica

BUS 41 to Porta San Pancrazio, 44, 710 along Via San Pancrazio

OPEN dawn to dusk

ADMISSION free, *casino* not open

WHEELCHAIRS yes, with assistance

REFRESHMENTS no

LAVATORIES no

In 1630 Pamphilo Pamphili bought a simple villa and some land on the Janiculum Hill, just outside the west of Rome, on the site of the Emperor Galba's garden (mid-first century AD). When Pamphilo died in 1639 he left a wife, Olimpia, and three sons. Olimpia was not a helpless widow and soon after her husband's death she began to lavish attention on his brother, Cardinal Giambattista Pamphili. Such was her influence over him that when he succeeded to the papal throne in 1644 as Innocent X she was dubbed 'the first *papessa* of Rome'. During Innocent's reign a decision was taken that allowed money from the Holy See to be used to enrich the pope's immediate family. With Olimpia at the helm, the Pamphili were to benefit enormously during Innocent's reign. Camillo, one of Olimpia's sons, decided to transform the family villa into a residence that befitted their new status.

Camillo's first choice of architect was Francesco Borromini. Sadly, Borromini's extravagant plans did not meet with his patron's approval. His intention had been to create a series of walled avenues that could be flooded for a number of hours each day so that Pamphili's visitors

lazio

could walk around the park in the morning and then retrace their journey by boat after lunch! Borromini was no doubt inspired by the convenient proximity of the city aqueduct. In the notes that accompanied his plans Borromini explained that they could be realised with little inconvenience to the citizens of Rome who 'would only have to lose their water for an hour each day'. He also intended to build a replica of the ark fitted with stalls: animals were to be purchased to live in it, though Borromini admitted that life-size replicas would substitute for some species. A statue of Innocent x was to stand in the garden, so placed that at the hour of his accession a ray of sun would touch the tips of his toes.

Camillo eventually commissioned Alessandro Algardi and Giovanni Francesco Grimaldi, who was a landscape painter. The original intention had been to extend the old villa but this was abandoned in favour of building the *casino*. The new building served as a setting for the Pamphili's extravagant receptions and parties, and it also housed the family's considerable collection of classical sculpture. The old villa remained virtually unchanged, although Algardi laid out gardens and an orange grove around it.

G B Falda's engraving of 1683 provides an accurate record of Algardi's layout. The regular plantation of trees and hedges that can still be seen in front of the *casino*'s main entrance formed the upper garden. The sunken garden to the rear of the building contained traditional geometric parterres arranged around a central fountain. It overlooked the lower garden, which was bounded by ilex woods and occupied by parterres, a large amphitheatre and an elaborate grotto set in the hill. Beyond the gardens the vast park was intersected by a series of avenues flanked by hedges and statues.

By the end of the seventeenth century the Pamphili family was extinct, and the property passed by marriage to the Doria of Genoa. In 1720 Gabriele Valvassori was commissioned to design the Fountain of the Tiber and the Fountain of Venus that were to stand outside the old villa. He also had a wall built around Algardi's orange grove. Later in the eighteenth century the nearby villas of Ferroni and Corsini were annexed to the property.

Early in the nineteenth century Prince Doria took an English wife, Mary Talbot. Gwendoline Talbot, her sister, was to marry the Borghese prince of the day. Under Mary's orders much of Algardi's garden was uprooted, making way for an 'English' park. She put a signature to the completed work by having her name inscribed in clipped cypress on the eastern slopes of the park.

During the Siege of Rome in 1849 the park was witness to some ferocious fighting between Napoleon III's forces, intent on defeating the republican government, and an army drawn from the populace of Rome, under the military leadership of Giuseppe Garibaldi. A neoclassical memorial to the dead was erected beyond the family villa. Before they sold the villa and park to the State in 1963, the Doria replaced all the fountains with copies, taking the originals with them.

The *casino* can be seen from the park's main entrance and it is a magnificent sight. The building is surmounted by a delicate balustrade, and its walls are decorated with ancient bas-reliefs set into pale stucco. From a distance it has a luminous and almost ethereal quality.

A path leads through the bleak periphery of the park and joins the carriage drive to the *casino*. The gate that marks the main entrance to the garden is closed and the drive must be followed till it emerges beside the retaining wall of the sunken garden. Between the flights of steps that linked the two gardens are seen the poor remains of Algardi's Grotto of Venus. The wall is decorated with the doves and lilies that were the emblems of the Pamphili.

The sunken garden is not open to the public. However, there is a marvellous view to be had by climbing the steps to the terrace above it. The garden is enclosed on one side by the villa and on the others by the retaining walls of the upper terraces. Niches set in the walls are adorned with statues. The *parterres de broderie* that replaced the original geometric beds are probably of the end of the seventeenth century. They are set out around a copy of a fountain by Pietro Tacca. Pots of lemons decorate the outer wall of the garden and the oblong pool that lies to one end of it. The pool also contains bronze fountains in the form of Pamphili lilies. Ducks and geese swim on it, and there is a tree that grows on a circular island at its centre.

The Roman climate does not favour lawns. Consequently, the 'English' park that replaced Algardi's lower parterre garden is a desolate sight. The sunken pit of the amphitheatre can still be seen. However, the niches in its semicircular wall are bare, and it is adorned only by Pamphili lilies and swags of *spugne*.

Algardi's grotto set in the hillside between the *casino* and the amphitheatre has recently been restored. There is an ornate nineteenth-century fountain at the centre of the lower garden, its marble bowl supported by satyrs carrying baskets of fruit on their heads.

It is important to remember that the *casino* and its gardens represent a very small part of the park, which once had a circumference of c. 10 kilometres. Wooded slopes extend to the south and west, giving way above the *casino* to a large area of level ground that was used as a *manège*. Below the trees that bound the *manège* is a short canal. A series of rustic cascades descend from the Fountain of the Lily to a small lake. This area was laid out at the end of the seventeenth century when the shores of the lake were used as a small hunting reserve. Today, the canal teems with tame coypu that come to the banks to be fed cold pasta and banana skins by passing children.

A copy of Bernini's beautiful Fountain of the Queen, better known as the *Lumaca,* or snail, stands in the meadow above the canal. Olimpia Pamphili is said to have persuaded Innocent that it was too small for its intended setting in Piazza Navona in Rome.

The family villa lies on the road that is the park's northern boundary. The walls still stand around what remains of Algardi's orange grove. Valvassori's Fountain of the Tiber is set in the wall opposite the villa. The air of desolation that haunts the park is concentrated in this corner.

NEAREST MAJOR TOWN Viterbo
MAIN FEATURES beautiful sixteenth-century garden, casino and water staircase
PRE-BOOKING no
OWNER the State
ADDRESS Piazza Farnese, I-01032 Caprarola; tel. +39 (0)761 646052
LOCATION Caprarola is c. 19 kilometres south-east of Viterbo. Follow signs for Ronciglione; after c. 15 kilometres turn off to Caprarola; the villa is conspicuous in the centre of town

OPEN 9.00–19.00; guided tours only every 15 minutes (weekdays), 30 minutes (weekends/public holidays); tours of casino and park at 10.00, 11.30, 15.00 (weekdays), 10.00, 15.00 (weekends/public holidays). The park and casino have been closed for some time for restoration – it is advisable to telephone beforehand
ADMISSION L4000, children free
WHEELCHAIRS no
REFRESHMENTS no
LAVATORIES yes

In 1556 Cardinal Alessandro 1 Farnese commissioned Giacomo Barozzi da Vignola to transform his uncle's partly built fortress at Caprarola, begun in 1532 and left untouched for 20 years, into a palace befitting the more settled times. Work began on the gardens behind the palazzo the following year, and in 1559 construction of the building itself got under way.

The sophistication and luxury of the palazzo were unparalleled, earning Alessandro a firm rebuke from Cardinal Carlo Borromeo. Told that the money would have been better spent on the poor, Alessandro (with a readier wit than his colleague at Villa Lante; page 314) replied to the effect that he had indeed given the money to them: they had earned it by the sweat of their brows.

Vignola died in 1573. One of the twin secret gardens was finished, and the palazzo nearly so. It is not certain whether Vignola himself planned the creation of a further garden in the hunting wood behind the palazzo. However, in 1584 the cardinal proceeded to build a delightful *casino* there, some of whose waterworks strongly recall Vignola's work at Bagnaia (page 314). The casino was probably designed by Giacomo del Duca. It was finished in 1586, 3 years before Alessandro's death. It is pleasant to think of him enjoying this enchanting place in his old age.

In 1620 the gardens around the casino were laid out afresh by Girolamo Rainaldi whose alterations included the rustication of the stonework, and the addition of the grottoes and *canephori,* the latter carved by Pietro Bernini.

The last of the Farnese died in 1731 and the villa passed to the Bourbons. They stripped it of its contents and left it to decay. In 1940 it was bought by the State and the casino later became an occasional residence for the President of Italy.

This enormous building towers over Caprarola. At first sight it is difficult to imagine a garden that would not be crushed into insignificance against a background of such overwhelming grandeur. The solution found to this problem was brilliantly simple. The main gardens were to be sufficiently distant from the palazzo for there not to be a conflict of attention. It is a pity that it is not known to what extent Vignola was responsible for this plan. Certainly, del Duca carefully followed Vignola's work at Villa Lante both in the design of the waterworks and the casino.

The palazzo is pentagonal in plan. The two square *giardini segreti,* a western winter garden and a northern summer garden, for which Vignola was responsible, lie behind it, each parallel to a different facet of the pentagon. As was customary, the cardinal had two sets of apart-

ments. One was for winter use and faced west, the other, facing north, was for the summer. Each set of rooms overlooks one of the gardens and is connected to it by a wooden bridge over the moat that surrounds the palazzo.

After walking through a maze of stairs and passages, a custodian showed us through the cardinal's dressing room and into the garden facing his winter apartments. Since the Second World War this has been replanted in the original pattern, with four green parterres surrounded by hedges of box, holly and laurel. A central avenue (once covered by a pergola) leads to the Fountain of the Rain in a grotto at the far end of the garden where water drips from the roof and the faces of satyrs emerge from the *spugne*-covered walls. In front of it the Farnese lily is laid out in mosaic. A balustraded terrace is above the grotto.

The garden facing the summer apartments was closed for restoration on our visit. It originally had flowerbeds and fruit trees. A nymphaeum at the far end contained the Fountain of Venus. Between the two *giardini segreti* is a raised terrace around which runs a rose pergola.

From the summer garden a path leads up into the hunting wood. As one strolls across the turf in the shade of the ancient chestnut trees the formality of the palazzo behind is forgotten. It is now that the garden springs its most delightful surprise. The path becomes a straight grassy pine avenue. In a sunny clearing at the far end the casino rises up in perfect harmony with its sylvan setting. It stands at the top of a short slope and is reached by shallow steps between rusticated walls. Down the middle of the steps runs a water staircase of intertwined dolphins. Grottoes are set into the retaining walls on either side.

Walking up the steps, with the sounds of water echoing from the walls on either side, one finds oneself in the small piazza at the head of the water staircase. Stairs sweep up and around the central fountain to the terrace above. The fountain is an extraordinary creation. Two enormous Tritons bearing cornucopias flank an urn as vast as any at Bomarzo (page 274). The urn is filled with water from a jet in the form of the Farnese lily. The water overflows into a lower basin, around the rim of which are set bowls from which spring further jets. There is a grotto behind the basin.

As one climbs the curving stairs, there are wall fountains in the form

of grotesque masks set in the side niches. At top is a small piazza. On either side the Farnese unicorns spout water into shells borne by kneeling Tritons. Beyond the piazza is the large, rectangular terrace around the casino planted as a formal garden with box parterres. On the low wall running around the terrace stand 28 tall *canephori*. Each has a vase on its head, and some hold animals in their arms. The pair at each corner face each other and hold hands. There is a charming story to the effect that each one is a portrait of one of the workmen employed in the construction of the garden.

Flights of steps decorated with water-spouting dolphins on either side of the casino lead up to the last terrace behind it. Here there is a fountain surrounded by shallow mosaic steps. The Farnese coat-of-arms is also laid out in mosaic. Beyond the fountain three low terraces recede towards the woods. They are planted with roses and the retaining walls are set with many fountains that sadly no longer function. Finally a gate decorated with nymphs astride unicorns opens to the forest outside.

giardini della landriana

NEAREST MAJOR TOWN Rome
MAIN FEATURES extensive modern garden designed in part by Russell Page, large collection of roses and exotic plants
PRE-BOOKING no
OWNER Lavinia Taverna
ADDRESS Via Campo di Carne 51, Tor San Lorenzo, I-00040 Ardea (Rome)
LOCATION take Via Pontina (ss148) south from Rome. Leave at the Ardea exit after c. 39 kilometres on the Via Ardeatina. Continue to Ardea and follow signs for the garden
OPEN Saturday to Sunday, April to October, guided tours on the hour, 10.00–12.00, 15.00–18.00; English-speaking guides available for groups on request
ADMISSION L10,000, children L5000
WHEELCHAIRS yes
REFRESHMENTS lunch can be provided for groups by prior arrangement
LAVATORIES yes

It has taken little more than 40 years to create La Landriana, one of the largest and most important modern gardens in Italy. The garden's history goes back to 1956 when Lavinia Taverna and her husband, the Marchese Gallerati Scotti, bought a derelict dairy farm 40 kilometres south of Rome. Their principal interest was in the pasture land and at first they gave little attention to the tumble-down house and derelict barns that had been thrown in with the sale. The land lay only 4 kilometres from the sea and was full of unexploded mines left over from the Second World War. The fields were raked by sea winds and over the years they had been stripped of any natural vegetation.

At first Lavinia's interest lay in alpines and other rock plants. Later she focused on plants from Australia, South Africa and California and found that exotic plants acclimatised well in the gentle coastal climate of La Landriana. By 1968 she already had a sizeable collection of exotics. At this point she met Russell Page, who at that time was liv-

ing in Italy and was designing English gardens for the Roman aristocracy. Page was commissioned to create a framework for the large but somewhat disparate plant collection.

Disciples of Page will find few traces of his work here. Taking courage from his design, Lavinia began almost at once to make the garden her own and has continued, with formidable creative energy, to expand and develop the site ever since. It now covers 10 hectares and has 32 separate 'rooms', each with its own distinct character. The planting has been planned to provide continuous interest from the depths of winter to the blazing height of summer. Every April, when the apple blossom is at its peak, La Landriana is the site of a garden festival. Primavera alla Landriana is Italy's equivalent of the Chelsea Flower Show. Gardening is undergoing a renaissance in Italy and with each passing year the spring festival attracts greater numbers of visitors.

There are at least 500 species of rose in the garden and during May they reach their crescendo. The 'Bonica' Walk, a cobbled road that was once a drive, stretches into the middle distance. To either side silver olive leaves float above the creamy pink flowers of 'Bonica' roses. This boldly repetitive design is underscored by a line of *Pittosporum tenuifolium* 'Silver Queen' clipped into neat globes, contrasting with an under planting of *Hebe* 'Mrs Winder'.

Beyond the 'Bonica' Walk lies the Orange Garden, the first of a series of garden rooms originally conceived by Page. The square beds were once planted with roses but after six years the soil was exhausted and Lavinia substituted the planting seen today. Bitter orange trees were placed at the centre of four of the beds. Severely clipped to resemble glossy, green lollipops, the trees are studded with brilliant fruit throughout the year. The corners of the beds are marked by globes of Cape myrtle (*Myrsine africana*). An under planting of *Pratia pendunculata* provides a splash of violet-blue each spring. The garden is given a less formal dimension by the softer shapes of *Acer platinoides* 'Globosum' that stand at the centre of the remaining beds.

The entrance to Page's Olive Garden is marked by a majestic cork oak. Enclosed by olives, the garden has beds arranged around two stone fountains. Page invited Lavinia to concoct her own planting scheme for this area. Today she describes them as wonderful carpets in which the same colours are repeated in different combinations. In April delicate yellow tulips sound the first note in a symphony of violet and yellow that will continue throughout the year. In May, the yellow of 'Friesia' roses and *Sisyrinchium striatum* coincide with the mauve heads of *Allium rosembachianum*. The warm air is laden with the scent of southernwood, bronze fennel and *Artemesia abrotanum.*

The White Walk is the name given to a gentle flight of steps below the Olive Garden. Here Lavinia's bold design leads the eye beyond the enclosed walk to the water of the lake below. Clipped laurel hedges line the steps and beds to each side are packed with 'Madame Alfred Carriére', 'Sea Foam' and 'Penelope' roses, their white flowers luminous against the dark leaves of the laurel.

In her excellent companion guide, Lavinia describes the Valley of the Roses as the most important part of the garden. Over the years she has assembled a massive collection of old and modern roses planted in free-form beds linked by grass paths. In May, when the roses are in full bloom and the air is aloud with the song of nightingales, one must thank the instinct that kept the Gallerati Scotti at La Landriana, slowly reclaiming and transforming the desolate landscape into a place of unique beauty.

NEAREST MAJOR TOWN Viterbo
MAIN FEATURES beautifully preserved
sixteenth-century garden, fine water
staircase and fountains
PRE-BOOKING no
OWNER the State
ADDRESS Via J Barozzi 71, I-01031
Bagnaia; tel.: +39 (0)761 288008
LOCATION Villa Lante is signposted
clearly from Viterbo by following the
SS204 towards Orte. Bagnaia is
4 kilometres east of Viterbo. In the
central piazza (XX Settembre) in
Bagnaia turn first right – the entrance
to the villa is at the end of the street
OPEN Monday to Friday, 9.00–an hour
before sunset; closed public holidays.
Accompanied tours only, every 30
minutes. The villas may be visited by
prior arrangement
ADMISSION L4000, children under
18 years free
WHEELCHAIRS no
REFRESHMENTS no
LAVATORIES no

Bagnaia, in the diocese of Viterbo, was for many years a place of retreat and recreation for its bishops. At the beginning of the sixteenth century the forest above the town, known as Monte Sant'Angelo, was enclosed to form a hunting wood. In 1514 the first building on the site, a small hunting lodge, was erected. This still stands in the park. In 1549 an aqueduct was built to convey water to both park and town.

In 1566 Cardinal Giovanni Francesco Gambara was appointed to the bishopric. It is almost certain that he commissioned Giacomo Barozzi da Vignola, then working at Caprarola (page 303), to draw up the design for his new residence.

The garden was completed by 1573. Both *palazzine* were included in the original plan. The first was completed and occupied by 1578. However, in 1579 Gambara's allowance was stopped, probably on the intervention of Cardinal Carlo Borromeo whose austere, if saintly, nature

is known to have been offended by the lavish spending of many of his colleagues. The creation of beauty was, in his view, no part of the proper function of a Prince of the Church. On the cardinal's advice Gambara went no further with his plans, and built a local hospital instead.

In 1587 Gambara died and the Vatican immediately took over the property. It was rented to his successor on the condition that on his death it should be left to the current pope's nephew, Cardinal Mon-

lazio

talto, who inherited in 1590. He proceeded to build the second *palazzina* and to make minor alterations to the layout of the garden. This included the great central fountain, to which he added the figures of the four Moors supporting the Montalto crest.

In 1640 work had begun in Rome on a new series of fortifications and this resulted in the loss of most of the garden of the villa belonging to the Lante family. In compensation they asked for the villa at Bagnaia, still owned by the Holy See. In 1655 they were granted the lease on a peppercorn rent, which eventually lasted for 200 years. They were given the freehold during the last century. In the seventeenth century a French member of the family was responsible for the *parterres de broderie* around the central fountain, which were originally simple square beds. The Lante left the villa in 1932. In 1953 it was bought by Angelo Cantoni, who made good the considerable war damage and brought the garden to its present wonderful condition. It is now owned by the State. The only regret is that visitors are given so short a time to appreciate it.

Villa Lante has a well-deserved reputation as the most beautiful of all the Roman gardens. Its modest scale, symmetry that is perfect without being daunting and the hundred variations of running water under the shade of its great plane trees combine to make it an unforgettable experience. Like many Roman estates, Villa Lante was intended for public as well as private enjoyment. Thus it has two entrances, one for the parterre garden and the other for general use for the park that surrounds the garden (and was once an extension of it). Entry is through the second gate. Set into the rising ground inside is the Fountain of Pegasus, who is emerging from an oval balustraded basin. From the wall behind herms spurt fine jets of water into the pool.

lazio

Just as at Tivoli (page 287), the garden of Villa Lante might have been read as easily as a piece of narrative verse by the sixteenth-century eye. Unlike the Este garden, however, the symbolism does not glorify an individual but retells the tale of man's ascent from the Golden Age to the Age of Civilisation, as recounted in Ovid's *Metamorphoses* (first century AD). Briefly, the park represents the free but primitive Golden Age, though the statues which indicate this have nearly all been lost or changed. Following this Age came the Flood, just as the water flows from the park to the Fountain of the Deluge. From here the water runs under the control of a great crayfish (a *gambero*, a pun on the cardinal's name and his personal emblem). Further on the Rivers Tiber and Arno, overlooking the dining terrace, make the land fruitful. The formal garden at the lowest level demonstrates the synthesis of Nature and Art. (For a detailed account of the iconography of the garden, see David R Coffin in the Bibliography.)

A flight of shallow steps to the left of the Fountain of Pegasus leads up to the gate into the lower garden. This is square and it contains *parterres de broderie* set around a large, square pool. There is a circular island in the centre reached by balustraded bridges from each side. On the island stand the travertine figures of four Moors holding aloft the Montalto crest, surmounted by a star spraying water. Four stone boats float on the pool, each manned by an *arquebusier* from whose weapons further jets of water once sprang.

The garden continues up the slope between the twin *palazzine*. The right-hand one is the earlier, erected by Gambara, and was used as the owner's residence. The Montalto *palazzina* was for formal receptions. Between the *palazzine* paths lead up to the next level. The Fountain of the Lights is set in the retaining wall and resembles a flight of steps to

the next level. Jets of water rise like candlesticks from little stone dishes along each step, hence its name. Grottoes to either side, currently under restoration, belong to Neptune and to Venus.

The next level forms the 'dining room' of the garden. The view from here is magnificent and looks over the parterre garden with the roofs of the town behind it and beyond that open countryside. In the centre of the terrace is a long stone table with a channel cut down its length, through which fresh water flows. Too high to sit at, the table was presumably used to cool wine after the Imperial Roman fashion. Behind the table is the Fountain of the Giants whose gods Tiber and Arno (strongly resembling the Neptune at Bomarzo) overlook the pool at the base of the fountain. Water overflows into the pool from a central basin supported by a triton. This in turn is fed by the claws of an enormous crayfish whose limbs border the water staircase above. They stretch all the way to the next terrace, where the mouth of the *gambero* pours out water between them.

Hedges enclose the uneven steps on either side of the water staircase. One emerges into a box-walled enclosure lined with stone benches. In the centre is the three-tiered Fountain of the Dolphins. *Giochi d'acqua* around the base of the fountain are still in use.

Behind this, great plane trees line the approach to the head of the garden. So old that many of them are little more than hollow trunks, they still cast a delightful green shade over the terrace. Behind them lies the last fountain, that of the Deluge. It is a tall fern-filled grotto with a central cascade pouring into a pool where two mossy dolphins swim. Enclosing it on either side are the two charming Pavilions of the Muses, frescoed inside with birds, flowers and musicians. There is a small *giardino segreto*, filled with roses, to the left.

NEAREST MAJOR TOWN Rome
MAIN FEATURES incomplete sixteenth-century garden designed by Raphael of great historic importance
PRE-BOOKING yes
OWNER the State (Ministero degli Affari Esteri)
ADDRESS Via di Villa Madama, I-00194 Rome; tel.: +39 (0)6 36911
LOCATION the villa, at the end of the
Via di Villa Madama, is not far from the Olympic Stadium in the north-west quarter of Rome. It is not easily reached by public transport
OPEN by prior arrangement through the Information Office
ADMISSION free
WHEELCHAIRS yes
REFRESHMENTS no
LAVATORIES yes

Despite the Villa Madama's brief and turbulent history, its importance to Roman garden architecture cannot be overestimated. It was one of the earliest buildings in which a return to the ancient Roman tradition was consciously attempted. Though incomplete, its influence can be traced in almost every subsequent Renaissance design.

The work was commissioned by Cardinal Giulio de'Medici. The plans were drawn up by Raphael Sanzio, and work began early in 1516. Following Raphael's death in 1520 it was continued by his colleagues Antonio da Sangallo, Giulio Romano and Giovanni da Udine. Work stopped the next year when the cardinal was compelled to return to Florence and was not resumed till 1524, after his election to the papacy as Clement VII. In a couple of years the villa was on the way to completion, and was already a meeting-place for the learned and the amusing among the pope's acquaintance.

Disaster struck when in 1527 Rome was brutally sacked by Charles V's Spanish army, which ran riot after the deaths of its generals. The villa was burned almost under the eyes of its unhappy owner, who was

lazio

effectively a prisoner in Castel Sant'Angelo and who could see smoke rising from it on the horizon. Though Clement later made good the damage to the building, he went no further. Too many of the friends with whom he had once enjoyed it lay murdered. It remains today as it stood before the sack.

On Clement's death in 1534 the villa was left to Ippolito de'Medici. When he died all his properties were confiscated by Paul III and in 1539 it passed to the his grand-daughter, Margaret of Austria, for whom it is named. In 1549 Paul died and the villa was restored to the Medici. Six years later Catherine de'Medici, Queen of France, gave it to Cardinal Alessandro Farnese.

With the extinction of the Farnese line during the eighteenth century, Villa Madama passed to the hands of the Bourbons and as with their other villas a long period of ruinous neglect resulted. The gardens were restored by a tenant at the beginning of the twentieth century using Sangallo's original drawings. Since 1960 it has been owned by the State and is used to hold receptions.

Raphael's original plans drew heavily on Pliny the Younger's famous description of his villa and garden by the sea at Laurentum, and on the scale of the remains of Imperial baths he knew when Superintendent of Roman Antiquities under Leo X. By following the ancient tradition Raphael hoped to create a place where garden and building would merge without abrupt transitions from 'inside' to 'outside'. The villa was to be built as, roughly speaking, a square block enclosing a great circular open courtyard. Having entered from the south-east face there would have been a choice of three exits from the courtyard. Each would lead through the villa to reveal a different aspect of the gardens. To the left a Roman amphitheatre was to have been excavated from

the hillside, while on the right the whole slope below the villa was to have been terraced. The villa was to lie at the junction of two perpendicular axes. The whole building was aligned with the Vatican to the south-east. A road was to run straight to it from the Ponte Milvio, the line being continued through the amphitheatre to join the Via Trionfale at the summit of Monte Mario above the villa.

lazio

Only half the building was completed, so that the wall of the central courtyard now forms the semicircular façade. Inside the villa the great north-west loggia is most gloriously frescoed with scenes from fables from Ovid's *Metamorphoses* by Giovanni da Udine, Giulio Romano and Baldassare Peruzzi. The loggia is now glassed in to preserve the frescoes, but it was originally open to the garden beyond.

This garden is known as the Giardino della Fontana and continues the axis towards the north-west. It is filled with clipped box parterres in rectangular patterns. Recently an attempt was made by the gardeners to introduce colour in this dark area by planting roses. However, the Soprintendenza had them removed on the grounds that they were anachronistic. Three niches are set into the west wall of the garden. The central one contains Giovanni da Udine's elephant-head fountain, said to have been copied from a classical original. The opposite side of the garden is open to a magnificent view east over Rome. Beneath the balustrade is a large oblong pool fed by fountains in the retaining wall. The wall at the far end of the garden has a gate flanked by two enormous stucco figures by the Florentine Baccio Bandinelli. Most of the garden statuary was looted during the Second World War, but these were evidently too big to move.

The gate leads into the hippodrome, so called from a reference to a similar feature in one of Pliny's letters, rather than from its function. Green parterres run down the centre, and long lines of cypresses create shaded walks down either side. There is an eighteenth-century nymphaeum at the far end. The garden is a place of great peace and beauty, and is well cared for by the gardeners. The curator, surely one of the happiest men in Rome, told us that nothing but the owls ever disturbed his night's rest. *Pax romana*.

NEAREST MAJOR TOWN Latina
MAIN FEATURES magnificent twentieth-century collection of indigenous and exotic plants, trees and shrubs set among medieval ruins on the banks of a river

PRE-BOOKING no

OWNER Fondazione R Caetani
ADDRESS Via Ninfina, 1-04010 Doganella di Ninfa
LOCATION Ninfa is c. 70 kilometres south-east of Rome. Take either the SS148 (quicker) or SS7. From the SS148 cut across to Cisterna at Montello, c. 55 kilometres from Rome. From Cisterna follow yellow tourist signs for Ninfa. At Doganella cross the main road. The entrance to the garden is on the right after c. 1 kilometre. If the lake and medieval tower come into view then the car park has been passed: it is before the garden entrance

OPEN April to November, first weekend of each month, third Sunday of April to June, 1 May. Guided tours only; as a limited number of tickets are sold each day it is best to buy them in advance from the Fondazione R Caetani, Palazzo Caetani, Via della Botteghe Oscure 32, 1-00186 Rome; tel. +39 (0)6 68803231. Tickets may also be bought from World Wildlife Lazio, Via Trinità dei Pellegrini 1, 1-00186 Rome; tel. +39 (0)6 6896522. In Latina, tickets may be bought from the EPT, Via Duca del Mare 19, 1-04100; tel.: +39 (0)773 498711

ADMISSION L10,000

WHEELCHAIRS yes, with assistance

REFRESHMENTS yes

LAVATORIES yes

Pliny the Younger, the ancient Roman administrator/lawyer, records a visit to the prosperous town of Ninfa in the first century AD when there was a temple sacred to the nymphs built over the spring of the River Nympheus. His account was recently confirmed when divers working on the bed of the lake beneath the castle keep found the remains of a classical temple.

lazio

By 1159 the town had seven churches and was encircled by double walls. Its site on the road between Rome and Naples made it a popular stopping place. In 1297, at the height of its prosperity, it was bought by Boniface VIII who gave it to his nephew, Pietro Caetani. It was he who built the structure that still serves to dam the lake and the castle that overlooked it. The town continued to flourish until disaster struck in 1382. Onorato Caetani, who was embroiled in the events of the Great Schism, declared Clement VII antipope, and Ninfa was razed to the ground as a result. The few survivors who stayed on in the ruined town soon fell victim to malaria. What was left of their shops and houses, and the remains of the fortified walls that surrounded them, was abandoned until the early years of this century. When Ferdinand Gregorovius, the German historian, visited Ninfa in the mid-nineteenth century, he commented: 'Truly this place looks even more charming than Pompeii, for there the houses stare like crumbling mummies dragged from the volcanic ashes. Over Ninfa waves a balmy sea of flowers'.

The transformation of the ruined town into a garden was the work of three women over about 90 years. The first to garden there was Ada Wilbraham Caetani, Duchess of Sermoneta and English wife of Duke Onorato Caetani. Stories of her eccentricities live on to this day: she is said to have organised obstacle courses for her guests at dinner parties, an unusual enough idea today, let alone at the end of the nineteenth century. Ada used to bring her six children to Ninfa for picnics and it was on these expeditions that she began to plant rose cuttings against the walls of the ruined buildings. A century later Ada's roses, recognisable by their massive stems, still thrive.

Ada's successor in the garden was Marguerite Chapin, Anglo-Amer-

ican wife of Duke Roffredo Caetani and founder of two brilliantly successful international literary magazines. She began work at Ninfa in 1932 and continued her passionate association with the garden until her death in 1958. During this period Ninfa was often the setting for informal picnics to which the duchess invited writers, poets, artists and foreign diplomats. During the 1930s, when the political climate in Italy was becoming ever more unpleasant, Ninfa represented an oasis of intellectual freedom.

The last of the Caetani to garden at Ninfa was Marguerite's daughter, Lelia. A gifted painter, Lelia's imagination ran riot, adding yet another layer to the accumulated depth and intensity of the planting. She married the Hon. Hubert Howard in 1951. The son of the British diplomat Esme Howard and Princess Giustiniani-Bandini, he threw himself into safeguarding Ninfa's future. Knowing that they would have no children, the couple set up the Fondazione R Caetani to administer Ninfa after their deaths. After a considerable battle, they established a conservation area around the garden, ensuring that industrial pollution would never destroy the river's precious purity.

Perhaps the most important thing that Lelia did for Ninfa was to find an heir to her ideas. From early childhood, Lauro Marchetti spent much of his life with Lelia, learning about the garden and absorbing the beliefs that underpinned her work there. Lelia died 20 years ago and Howard's death a decade later left Marchetti as Ninfa's custodian. The garden continues to flourish and expand seamlessly into adjoining land. Marchetti's light touch may have been learnt from Lelia, but by now it has become instinctive. The delicate balance between cultivation and the flowering wilderness bears witness to a rare sensitivity. The vital work of the Foundation has ensured the continued existence

of the garden, but it is Marchetti who must be thanked for preserving the spirit of the place. Under such care, Ninfa will never lose its focus.

Visitors to Ninfa enter a world apart. The garden opens out among the rambling streets and ruined buildings of the medieval town. The keep of Caetani's castle still towers over the garden, but it is empty now, except for a flock of doves that circle above it and make their nests between its grey stones.

Ninfa's roses are sublime. In late spring, surely the ideal time to visit the garden, the buildings of the ruined town appear and then vanish again beneath cascades of roses, summer jasmin with its heady scent, wisteria and clematis. There are more than 200 species of rose in the garden – many unidentifiable. They seem to thrive in the gentle climate, rampaging over fallen rocks, hurling themselves up walls and through the branches of trees.

Marguerite was passionate about the English rose. In 1949 alone she ordered 128 different species from the Hillier nursery in Winchester, Hampshire. (This was the beginning of an association with the Hilliers that was to continue for more than 30 years.) Marguerite particularly loved the *Rosa chinensis* 'mutabilis'. She planted it all over the garden and today it lends continuity to the fluid planting.

Marguerite also loved the flowering cherry. In 1960 she planted five different species in the area known as the Piazza delle Glorie, close to the ruined nave of San Biagio. In spring the walls of the church rise out of a sea of translucent cherry blossom. There are 20 different species of cherry in the garden. Some are planted along the banks of the river and their blossom is reflected in the water, transforming it into a blur of brilliant colour. The sound of water penetrates all but the furthest reaches of the garden. Ice cold and miraculously clear, the river rushes over vivid green weeds, dragging shoals of trout sideways across the current. Its course is punctuated by monumental stands of Columbian gunnera and brilliant yellow flag iris. The massive flowers of a wistaria hang voluptuously from an ancient wooden bridge, trailing their tips in the water.

The garden is threaded with numerous powerful little streams. The shining ribbons of water are often flush with the mown grass. In places the stream is channelled to create a tiny waterfall, in others it crosses over itself in a minute aqueduct. A larger stream meanders through a grove of exquisite birch. In late spring the perfect, waxy flowers of the arum lily pack the stream bed, seeming to recede into infinity among the silver trunks of the birches. The only place in the garden where the water lies still is in the limpid, mysterious pool at the centre of the towering grove of bamboo.

NEAREST MAJOR TOWN Rome

MAIN FEATURES nineteenth-century garden with sixteenth-century elements in the grounds of the Presidential palace

PRE-BOOKING yes

OWNER the State

ADDRESS Via del Quirinale, I-00187 Rome

LOCATION in the centre of Rome, the garden entrance is on Via del Quirinale

OPEN second and fourth Sundays of each month; telephone for additional information: +39 (0)6 46991

ADMISSION entrance fee payable (by arrangement)

WHEELCHAIRS yes

REFRESHMENTS no

LAVATORIES yes

During the fifteenth century Cardinal Carafa built a small villa on his family land on the Quirinal Hill in Rome, known at that time as Monte Cavallo. In 1550 it was rented by Cardinal Ippolito d'Este. He had been frustrated in his papal ambitions but was still in need of a Roman residence while he considered the development of his future home at Tivoli (page 287). The first garden on the site was laid out between 1550 and 1554 by Girolamo da Carpi. In 1560 Pius IV gave the cardinal an adjoining estate, and he began to extend both villa and garden.

In 1572 Ippolito died, and the property passed to his nephew Luigi d'Este. He preferred spending his time at Tivoli and offered the use of the villa to the new pope, Gregory XIII. Gregory was enthusiastic about the situation, later described by the eighteenth-century diarist John Evelyn as 'most excellent for ayre and prospect'. The open and still rural hill was a far healthier place than the low-lying area by the Tiber. Gregory made substantial alterations to the villa and also increased the water supply to the gardens.

In 1585 Gregory died; he requested that the improved property should be returned to Luigi. Instead his successor Sixtus V bought the land from the Carafa, who were still the landlords. He had the villa enlarged yet again by Domenico Fontana. Subsequent popes transformed the villa into the palazzo seen today. Several architects were employed, including Carlo Maderno and Gianlorenzo Bernini. The great Organ Fountain beneath the palazzo was built by Giovanni Fontana in 1596.

By 1670 the garden was laid out as 60 square parterres with intersecting avenues of cypress. This rather monotonous plan survived largely unaltered until the nineteenth century, when the great central avenue was cut through the grounds. The delightful summerhouse was added in 1741.

From the time of Sixtus onwards the palazzo became the principal papal residence and was occupied by 29 popes. Twenty-two of them died there. Curiously, each in turn bequeathed his heart and viscera to the church of SS Vincent and Anastasius. In 1870 the property was forcibly taken over by the Kingdom of Italy, and now serves as the Presidential palace.

The gardens can roughly be divided into two areas: the English garden and the *giardino all'italiana*. It is still possible to trace some of the sixteenth-century layout of the latter, though it has been radically transformed by its many owners. It is entered through what was once the stable block. Once past the magnificent presidential guards one finds oneself between the two gardens. They are divided by lawns and a wide gravel path with a central fountain. This was laid out during the nineteenth century under Gregory XVI. The finest of the garden's many palm trees grow in this area, some dating from 1736. Unfortunately several succumbed to the bitter winter of 1985.

On either side of the garden are immense hedges of bay and laurel. Ten years ago many of the hedges were in a very poor state, and the director of the garden had them lowered by c. 3 metres. Behind the hedges are ilexes of enormous age, several of which are known to have been planted during the tenure of Ippolito. On the right is the 'English' garden, planted with palm and maritime pine. Flower-filled Roman sarcophagi line the paths. At the centre is a superb plane tree, claimed to be the oldest in Italy.

The *giardino all'italiana* lies to the left. Here as elsewhere the hedges surrounding the repetitive square parterres of the seventeenth-century garden have grown to enormous heights. They have been left to form a fascinating and mysterious set of interconnected garden rooms. Each has stone benches where one can sit in deep shade gazing at the square of blue sky above. Arches cut through the hedges give sudden exciting glimpses of statues and fountains. An avenue through the centre of this area is lined with *commedia dell'arte* figures, including one of a cobbler using his shoe to separate two quarrelling pigs.

Beyond this garden lies the delightful summer- or coffee house built in 1741 for the meeting of Benedict XIV and Charles III of the Two Sicilies. Classical busts line the roof, while others stand on tall columns before it. The Fountain of Venus is in front of the coffee house and, unusually for Italy, there is also a handsome sundial said to have been designed by Francesco Borromini for Urban VIII in 1628. The base bears the Cybo crest. A garden room to the right of the coffee house contains a rustic fountain with spouting dolphins and stone turtles. *Giochi d'acqua* spurt up on all sides, enclosing the victim in a ring of spray. At the far end of the garden is the maze, added in the nineteenth century.

There is a raised terrace at the right-hand end of the palace. From

here one can look down at the enormous grotto containing the Organ Fountain. This is currently undergoing a long-awaited restoration. It was originally prepared in 1565 to contain Apollo and the Muses. The hydraulic organ was added in 1596. A recess to one side has a life-sized figure of Vulcan at his forge, with Cupid working the bellows.

Following the transition from monarchy to republic there was a lengthy period during which the gardens were not developed; however, they are now being beautifully maintained. The present director recognises that it would be pointless to attempt a return to the Renaissance layout and he is seeking to restore the gardens to their early nineteenth-century appearance.

NEAREST MAJOR town Rome
MAIN FEATURES Papal gardens since the fifteenth century, beautiful sixteenth-century *casino*
PRE-BOOKING no (see below)
OWNER Vatican State
LOCATION the ticket-office is close to St Peter's (on the left as one faces the basilica). For the Cortile del Belvedere, the entrance is as for the Vatican Museums, c. 400 metres round the Vatican walls to the right
OPEN December to March, guided tours twice a week on request; one tour is always on a Saturday; April to October, guided tours Monday, Tuesday, Thursday to Saturday, 10.00 (except festival days); Vatican Museums, 9.00–13.00. It is not always possible to enter the Cortile della Pigna and Cortile del Belvedere, though they can be seen from the museum windows
ADMISSION L18,000 for a two-hour guided tour
WHEELCHAIRS yes
REFRESHMENTS yes
LAVATORIES yes

It was not until the Middle Ages that the Vatican became the permanent home of the papacy. The fourth-century basilica of St Peter stood in open countryside until Leo IV enclosed it by fortifications between 848 and 852. During the thirteenth century the first palace was built near the old Basilica of Constantine. The first references to a garden date from this time; lawns and an orchard are mentioned. There was also a garden for medicinal herbs.

Following the return of the papacy from its exile in Avignon in 1377 major changes began to take place. The fifteenth century saw the completion of the palace, the construction of the Sistine Chapel and the proposals for the rebuilding of St Peter's. More importantly for the history of gardens it also saw the construction of the Villa Belvedere (also known as the Palazzetto), built by Innocent VIII in 1485. It stood on a

hill just outside the Leonine walls to the north of the basilica. The villa, turning its back firmly on the Vatican, was used as a retreat by the pope, who suffered from very poor health.

Innocent's court was dominated by the powerful figure of Cardinal Giuliano della Rovere, already described as 'Pope and more than Pope'. As soon as he was elected as Julius II in 1503 he began the greatest building programme the Vatican had yet seen. Most famous of his works is, of course, the rebuilding of St Peter's. He was a great collector of antiquities and had a fondness for the Villa Belvedere. In 1504, he commissioned Donato Bramante to produce a design to link the palace and villa, enabling the latter to display his collection of statues.

The area between the two buildings consisted of c. 350 metres of rising ground. Bramante's solution was to enclose the ground by extending wings from each end of the palace towards the villa. The resulting rectangular space was known as the Cortile del Belvedere and probably derived from descriptions of ancient villas and the on-site remains of the Naumachia Traiani (first century AD). A balustraded walk (the 'Stradone') ran along the top of each wing. The lowest area was an arena overlooked by a stepped amphitheatre beneath the façade of the palace. Half way along, a series of ramps and terraces ran between the two wings. These provided additional seating for spectators as well as giving access to a large formal garden at the top. At the far end of this garden the rectangle was completed by a two-storey loggia running from side to side. The focus of the whole conception was provided by a great exedra in the centre of the loggia. The villa remained a private place on the far side of the loggia, the space between the two buildings becoming a courtyard where Julius' statues could be displayed. This courtyard was greatly altered in the eighteenth century, but must have been most beautiful. It was planted with a grove of orange trees, and was filled with fountains. Julius wished his collection to be open to the public: Bramante's famous spiral staircase was built therefore to give public access to the courtyard without the necessity of entering through the palace.

This magnificently imaginative garden no longer exists. No apologies are given for describing it at length, for it and its successor Villa Madama (page 320) created an entirely new way of thinking about garden landscapes. The Belvedere courtyard, with its lavish use of fountains and deliberate placing of sculpture, was both a harking back to Roman antiquity and a model for all subsequent Italian gardens. In 1585 the Vatican Library was built across the middle of the garden, destroying its proportions. Later in the nineteenth century the Braccio Nuovo (part of the museum) was also built across the garden, resulting in the loss of the terraces. The 'Cortile del Belvedere' now refers only to the lower courtyard, used as a car park. The formal upper garden has become a dull expanse of grass called the Cortile della Pigna. They can both be seen while visiting the Vatican Museums, and in fact were meant to be viewed to their best advantage from the papal apartments, but it is perhaps best just to look at contemporary engravings of the garden at its peak.

There is another Vatican building of great importance in the context of gardens, the Casino of Pius IV, or Villa Pia. Begun in 1558 by Pirro Ligorio for Paul IV, who died soon after its commencement, it was completed under the Medici Pius IV, who took particular pleasure in it.

The subsequent history of these gardens is one of constant change, as each incumbent in turn left his mark. With the creation of the Vatican State in 1929 a great deal of building took place. One loss was the

Square Garden. This lay to the west of the Cortile della Pigna. It had originally been created as a secret garden during the 1540s for Paul III. It was walled and had four square parterres divided by *berceaux*.

To visit these gardens it is, sadly, no longer necessary to obtain a letter of introduction from a cardinal, and then to have it franked by the Vatican major-domo. However, ease of entry perhaps compensates for a little vanished romance. Space does not allow us to compete with the excellent and comprehensive official guidebook, so this description will be restricted to the major features of the garden.

The tour begins by following the Viale dell'Osservatorio through the most recently laid-out section of the grounds. It winds up the hill to the Leonine walls, which until 1929 marked the limit of the gardens. The central tower was built in 848 for defence against the Saracens, and withstood a French siege a millennium later. Below the Broadcasting Centre is the Giardino all'italiana, with two simple fountains and box parterres. It replaces the vanished Square Garden. The Giardino all'inglese, at the northern end of the walls, is in the form of an attractive oak wood filled with fountains. Beyond this is the Fontana dell'Aquilone (great eagle) whose impressive flow of water comes by way of Trajan's first century AD aqueduct from Lake Braccione, 32 kilometres away. The aqueduct was restored by Paul V and the fountain was built in 1611 by the Dutch architect Johann van Santen (Giovanni Vansanzio) to commemorate the restoration. The water flows from here through many other fountains, culminating in St Peter's Square. The eagle and the water-spouting dragons are references to Paul V's Borghese crest.

The Casino of Pius IV is down the slope from the fountain. The grace and charm of this perfect garden retreat are almost matchless. Its only possible equal is the Casino at Caprarola, which it predates by nearly 25 years (page 303). It houses the Papal Academy of Science, and special permission is needed to see the interior (inquire at the ticket-office). It takes the form of a small *casino* and open loggias that face each other across an oval courtyard. Both structures are richly decorated with stucco reliefs, mosaic and frescos. It was built at a time when a sincere Christian faith went hand-in-hand with an open-minded Renaissance humanism. This is reflected by the use of scenes from classical mythology for exterior decoration, and of religious imagery for the interior. This happy balance did not last long for in 1569 the reforming Pius V disposed of nearly all the classical statues decorating the Casino (and banished visitors from the fine collection of statues in the Belvedere).

The parterres that once radiated from the Casino have long gone. There is now a small eighteenth-century sunken piazza to the east that gives a marvellous view of the loggia rising from the pool at its feet. The piazza is filled with the sound of the water flowing into the pool on either side of the loggia. Above the water sits an ancient statue of Cybele. The gay mosaic panels on either side of her, though not original, are perfectly in keeping with the spirit of the building. They replace four stucco caryatids removed during a nineteenth-century restoration. The work was probably done by the Vatican School of Mosaic, whose building stands in the grounds.

campania

Campania is the most southerly of the mainland regions covered by this book. It is mostly low-lying and is extremely fertile. Under Roman rule it earnt the reputation of an earthly paradise. Its beautiful coast was lined with magnificent villas and gardens. In the towns the houses were built around smaller, domestic gardens, similar to those in the ruins of Pompeii.

During the eleventh century southern Italy was conquered by the Normans. Though they destroyed the beautiful Sicilian pleasure gardens of their Muslim predecessors, when building gardens themselves they chose to adopt the Islamic style. This tradition was brought to Naples and the mainland by the Frederick II in the thirteenth century. He had grown up in the court at Palermo, and he built gardens around his castles throughout southern Italy.

Royal gardens continued to be laid out in Campania throughout the fourteenth and fifteenth centuries. Those at Poggio Reale were designed at the end of the fifteenth century for the Crown Prince of Naples. They so impressed Charles VIII of France that he took a Neapolitan gardener home with him to design Italian gardens at Amboise and Blois.

NEAREST MAJOR TOWN Caserta

MAIN FEATURES vast eighteenth-century royal garden in the centre of town

PRE-BOOKING no

OWNER the State

ADDRESS Viale Dohuet 2/a, I-81100 Caserta; tel.: +39 (0)823 321400

LOCATION the palazzo lies in the centre of Caserta, on the left as you enter the town from the A2. Note that a bus runs the length of the garden every 30 minutes

OPEN garden 9.00–dusk; palazzo, Monday to Friday, 9.00–13.30, Saturday and Sunday, 9.00–13.00

ADMISSION garden L4000, palazzo L8000 (free to children under 18 years of age)

WHEELCHAIRS yes

REFRESHMENTS yes

LAVATORIES yes

Carlo III became the first Bourbon ruler of the Kingdom of the Two Sicilies in 1734. He was a great huntsman, and from the first he used to ride out from Naples to the woods of Caserta. He became so fond of the place that he eventually decided that it should be transformed into the new capital of his kingdom. He expelled the Caetani, who had been its rulers, and in 1751 commissioned Luigi Vanvitelli to draw up plans for a new town, a gargantuan palace and a garden.

By the end of 1751 Vanvitelli had already set to work on staking out an extension to the existing *barco*. In 1756 he published his plans as *Dichiarazione dei Disegni del Real Palazzo di Caserta*. The area immediately in front of the palace was to be laid out as a series of enormous *parterres de broderie*, while the rest of the garden was divided up into a series of garden rooms decorated with fountains. There was to be a pool with a circular island, an orchard and a gazebo on the crest of the hill opposite the palace. The plans show Carlo's hunting wood, intersected by a series of wide rides and included in the layout of the garden.

campania

Very little of the original plan for Caserta was realised. In 1759 Carlo III left Italy to become king of Spain. He made his Italian possessions over to his 8-year-old son, Ferdinando (later Ferdinando V). Vanvitelli continued to work but his attention was devoted largely to the palazzo and the problem of finding sufficient water for the garden. The aqueduct that he had begun in 1753 was finally completed in 1762. It brought water more than 32 kilometres to the site. In 1770 he turned his attention to the garden once more, but he died three years later.

Carlo Vanvitelli took over after his father's death and worked for Ferdinando. It is to him that the garden should rightly be attributed. In 1777 the canal was excavated and the embankments built for the ramps that enclose the Fountain of Juno. Turf seeded in the royal cowsheds was laid down to either side of the canal the following year.

Between 1785 and 1800 the English garden that lies east of the Fountain of Diana was created. This was conceived by Sir William Hamilton, then British minister to Ferdinand. With the king's blessing Hamilton sought the assistance of Sir Joseph Banks – already a famous botanist and President of the Royal Society. He introduced Hamilton to Joseph Gräefer who was soon appointed as head gardener at Caserta. Gräefer later laid out Admiral Lord Nelson's garden at Castello di Maniace in Sicily (page 372).

In 1838 De Lillo was employed to lay out a flower garden and a *manège* to the right of the palace. The area in front of the building was left untouched. By this time open lawns were far more fashionable than Vanvitelli's elaborate *parterres de broderie*. Work on the gardens continued till 1860, when the property passed to the House of Savoy. During the events that surrounded the Unification of Italy the palace was plundered and for many years the gardens were neglected.

The gardens at Caserta were part of massive and unrealised plan by which the palace was to be linked to Naples. An avenue flanked by canals was to be laid out along the route of the ancient Via Appia. A section of the road was completed before Carlo III's departure for Spain but the plan was soon abandoned. However, something of the effect that Vanvitelli intended can be appreciated from the grotto at the top of the water staircase. The straight line of the canal gives way to a road that continues through the massive portico of the palace and stretches beyond it to the horizon.

Vanvitelli's canal is punctuated by sculpted scenes from Ovid's *Metamorphoses* (first century AD)and divided by shallow cascades. The layout represents a gradual progression from the cultivated to the wild and culminates in the rough-hewn water staircase that climbs the hill about 3 kilometres from the palace.

If grandeur could be achieved by scale alone, then Vanvitelli's aim would have been realised. However, the absence of any real sense of proportion reduces the impact of the vast garden. The groves of ilex and camphor that stand to each side of the canal deprive it of the width that might have balanced its enormous length. The sculptures, which should create the climax of the design, dwindle into insignificance and are virtually invisible from the windows of the palace.

After its 32-kilometre journey through pipes and aqueducts, the water on which the garden relies for its effect is released at the top of the water staircase. Vanvitelli intended that it should eventually pass under the palace and emerge in the two canals that were to flank the Via Appia to Naples. A foaming cascade pours down the staircase, creating a suitably dramatic background for Paolo Persico's vivid sculptures of Diana and Actaeon. The unfortunate huntsman has just been turned into a stag. His dogs crowd around him in confusion and Diana, surrounded by her nymphs, looks across the water from the safety of her own island.

The water from the Fountain of Diana disappears underground below the pool, and then re-emerges to form the long basin of the Fountain of Venus. Gaetano Salamone executed Venus and her nymphs bidding farewell to Adonis in 1780. One of the nymphs is playing with Adonis' hunting dog and the wild boar that is destined to kill him appears to be waiting expectantly. The heads of other wild animals adorn the pool from end to end.

Beyond the fountain the water disappears underground again and emerges beneath Ceres and her court. It also flows to either side of the goddess from the upturned amphorae of two Tritons. Ceres' bronze wheat sheaf disappeared long ago but the putto sitting to one side of her still holds a medallion displaying the Trinacria, the emblem of Sicily. The pool is divided by another water staircase and the shallow steps are decorated with a series of different faces.

Once again the water disappears. This time it is spanned by the road at the Bridge of Hercules. It emerges as a magnificent cascade, which descends to the Fountain of Juno and Aeolus, a semicircular fountain representing the climax of the garden. The sculptures were executed by Angelo Brunelli, Andrea Violani, Persico and Salamone. Juno was to have sat in the middle of the great pool in a carriage drawn by peacocks. Aeolus is at the centre of the scene, sitting with his back to the Palace of the Winds. The winds themselves, newly released, writhe and squirm on the rocks to either side of him. Bas-reliefs set above four of the arched doorways of the 'palace' represent Jupiter and the goddesses, the marriage of Thetis and Peleus, the Judgement of Paris, and

campania

the marriage of Paris and Helen. The fountain is enclosed by two curving ramps decorated with statues.

The financial constraints that prevented the completion of the Fountain of Juno also made their mark on the Fountain of the Dolphins. The three dolphins that spit water into the final pool are very modest in comparison with the extravagant compositions of the other fountains. Beyond their pool the road stretches away towards the palace, interrupted only by the simple Fontana Margherita, which is decorated with a single basket of flowers.

The grand *peschiera* lies to the west of the central axis on a level with the Dolphin Fountain. Ferdinand v's little retreat, the 'Castellucio', is also in this area.

NEAREST MAJOR TOWN Ravello
MAIN FEATURES twentieth-century villa and garden in a spectacular coastal location
PRE-BOOKING no
OWNER Signore Marco Willeumier
ADDRESS Via S Chiara 26, I-84010 Ravello; tel.: +39 (0)89 857459
LOCATION well signposted from the centre of Ravello. Can only be reached on foot but it is a steep climb and there are several flights of steps
OPEN 9.00–dusk
ADMISSION L5000
WHEELCHAIRS no
REFRESHMENTS yes
LAVATORIES yes

At first glance Villa Cimbrone appears a fortified mediaeval palace built in the same Moorish style as the courtyard at Villa Rufolo (page 358). It may come as a surprise to know that the villa and garden were both created in the twentieth century. The land on which they stand was bought in 1904 by Ernest Beckett, an Englishman, who was soon Lord Grimthorpe. He is said to have paid L100 for a ruined farmhouse, wood, walnut grove, vineyard and magnificent view over the Gulf of Salerno. Grimthorpe chose not to employ a qualified architect. He enlisted the help of a local tailor, Nicola Mansi, with whom he spent the next 15 years creating the villa and garden. He died in 1917, a couple of years after its completion.

In 1915 Grimthorpe's sister bought the land below the belvedere and employed Mansi to build a smaller house for her family. The little villa was called The Rondinaia, or 'swallow's nest', and for many years it was the home of the American writer Gore Vidal.

Villa Cimbrone stayed in the family until 1960, when it was sold to its present owner by Grimthorpe's daughter. Marco Willeumier had known Lord Grimthorpe and his family for many years, and they were

most anxious that he should take it over. The beautiful condition of the garden today serves as ample explanation for their anxiety. Willeumier's grandfather came to Ravello from Switzerland. He opened The Palombo, the first hotel on the Amalfi coast. It is still owned by the family, and Marco has extended the business by opening part of Villa Cimbrone to guests.

Visitors to Villa Cimbrone must find their way through the back streets of Ravello to an impressive 'medieval' portal, apparently built to withstand cannon balls and battering rams alike. A little door set in the massive structure of the gate leads directly to the garden. The shady courtyard of the villa lies to the left, and beyond it are steps leading down to the crypt.

The garden is surrounded by terraced hillsides, and Grimthorpe seems to have felt no temptation to impose this traditional form on the sloping site of his garden. He was content to divide it simply between a lower and an upper garden, and an area of wooded hillside intersected by winding paths. Each level was built to frame a different aspect of the magnificent view.

On entering, one's eye is drawn at once along a straight walk leading from the villa to a magnificent terrace overlooking the sea. It is flanked by ornate walls, shaded in part by a pergola of vines, and spanned by a bridge that links the two levels of the garden. Beyond the walk a circular belvedere shelters a statue of Ceres silhouetted against the sea. The terrace is perched more than 300 metres above the sea, which seems to stretch to infinity beyond the classical busts that adorn the wall.

A winding path leads down the hill behind the terrace, and into the oak and chestnut woods. There is a neo-classical building, the Temple

of Bacchus, built on a ledge below the terrace. The bronze figure of Bacchus is a copy of a well-known classical statue at the Civic Museum in Naples. Grimthorpe's ashes are buried beneath it.

A natural cave further down the hillside contains an eighteenth-century statue of Eve. The cave's rugged walls create a striking setting for her pale figure.

The upper garden may be reached from the woods by way of the fine cypress avenue that leads to the rose garden. While the sea forms a background for the lower garden, this area is designed to frame the impressive peaks of the mountains. It is bounded by a line of maritime pines and is divided into two distinct areas by a decorative wall. The inner garden, which is enclosed by the wall, is filled with beds of roses set out around a sundial. The outer garden provides a setting for a series of classical figures – made to appear authentic by the effects of wind and weather. A seat set into the far wall bears a quotation from the *Rubaiyat of Omar Khayyam*.

Between the rose garden and villa is a charming summerhouse built in the same style as the villa and decorated with colourful tiles. It stands in a lovely secret garden, which is filled with a regular pattern of beds laid out around an eighteenth-century fountain. A curious collection of twentieth-century bronzes and mock medieval columns stand in front of the summerhouse.

NEAREST MAJOR TOWN Ravello
MAIN FEATURES thirteenth-century
Moresque courtyard garden in the
centre of Ravello, views over Gulf of
Salerno
PRE-BOOKING no
OWNER the State
ADDRESS Piazza Vescovado, I-84010
Ravello; tel.: +39 (0)89 857866

LOCATION entrance on the piazza in the
centre of Ravello
OPEN June to September, 9.30–13.00,
15.00–19.00; October to May,
9.30–13.00, 15.00–17.00
ADMISSION L4000, children L2000;
free on Thursday
WHEELCHAIRS yes, for courtyard only
REFRESHMENTS no
LAVATORIES no

Villa Rufolo was built by the wealthy Rufolo princes of the thirteenth century. The family's prosperity originally derived from trade. Their ships travelled all over the Mediterranean, and their principal imports were luxurious goods from the East.

The Rufolo reached the height of their splendour when they became bankers to Carlo I, the Angevin king who ruled Naples between 1266 and 1285. By the beginning of the fifteenth century the family had died out. However, a fragment of their garden survives, representing a precious relic of the period in which the Islamic tradition shaped the gardens of Naples and Sicily.

Between the fifteenth and seventeenth centuries the palace belonged to the Confalone and Muscettola families. In the eighteenth century it passed to the d'Afflitto, whose renovation of the villa destroyed some of its original features.

In 1851 a Scottish botanist called Francis Neville Reid bought Palazzo Rufolo, and entrusted its restoration to Michele Ruggiero, who was supervising the excavations at Pompei at the time. Reid cre-

ated the modern garden is laid out between the medieval buildings and the fine terrace that overlooks the sea. It is said that Wagner's vision of the magic garden in *Parsifal* came to him while visiting here in 1880.

In 1974 the property was bought by the local tourist board. A small museum was created in 1982.

Villa Rufolo commands a view of the Gulf of Salerno. It has two towers, one that served as a lookout, and another that was an ornamental addition to the gateway marking the entrance to the garden. It is flanked by two fierce crocodiles. Two more monsters look down on the entrance to the courtyard. Their gaping mouths once served to extinguish the flaming torches of guests before they entered the palace.

The courtyard consists of a colonnade surmounted by a delightful loggia. Slender columns are arranged in pairs to either side of the loggia's elaborate arches. The wall above is decorated with Moorish arabesques. Unfortunately, its beauty is somewhat marred by the massive buttresses inserted after it was badly damaged by storms in 1713.

Originally, pots of oranges, lemons and flowering plants adorned the garden. The air was cooled by a central fountain, and the colonnade offered deep pools of shade. This idyllic place would have been unimaginable in the castles of central or northern Italy.

The rest of the garden dates from the nineteenth century, and is laid out on two levels. The open loggia that overlooks the sea on the lower level is thought to have served as an *al fresco* dining room.

sicily (sicilia)

The idea of the pleasure garden (as opposed to the functional monastic garden of the early Middle Ages) originated in Sicily and spread to the rest of Italy. From the sixth to the twelfth centuries the island was subject to Eastern influences, being first under the rule of Byzantium and later belonging to the Saracens. It was they who introduced the orange and lemon trees that are today as necessary to a garden in Italy as is the rose to an English garden. In 1091 Sicily fell to the Normans under Roger I. Although they destroyed the Arab settlements, the Normans accepted much of the culture they found and were soon known as 'baptised sultans' and developed a style of architecture sometimes known as Sicilian-Norman. A number of buildings in this idiom survive, such as the Palazzo della Zisa in Palermo; all traces of the gardens surrounding them have disappeared. From contemporary descriptions it seems that the gardens conformed to the Islamic style, as seen in the Alcazar in Seville, where an enclosed park is filled with small pavilions and kiosks, sometimes surrounded by water and equipped with fountains. The greatest ruler of this period was Frederick II, known to have laid out gardens around his hunting lodges and palaces.

There are relatively few public gardens worth visiting in Sicily today, though the nineteenth century saw a renaissance of interest. In the interior of the island a long tradition of absentee landlords resulted in sadly neglected estates. On the coast, with its favourable climate, gardens are certainly in the making which in a few years' time will merit attention.

NEAREST MAJOR TOWN Palermo
MAIN FEATURES eighteenth-century
pavilions, statues
PRE-BOOKING no
OWNER Città del Palermo
ADDRESS Via Lincoln, I-90133
Palermo

LOCATION beside the Orto Botanico
(page 369), a 5-minute walk from
the central railway station
OPEN dawn to dusk
ADMISSION free
WHEELCHAIRS yes
REFRESHMENTS yes
LAVATORIES no

Though little-known outside Palermo, Villa Giulia stands as a landmark in civic planning as being the first public garden in Italy. It was originally known as the Villa del Popolo. It takes its present name from Giulia d'Avalos, wife of Marcantonio Colonna, Prince of Stigliano, who oversaw its construction. Apparently a decree had to be passed by the Senate to allow the people's park to be renamed in this way. This caused some disturbance in the city, but the park proved so popular that the prince was forgiven and his wife's memory has remained intact. (It is occasionally referred to as Villa Flora; the name said to have been given by the poet Johann Wolfgang von Goethe after his visit in 1786.) The garden was laid out by Nicolò Palma from 1777.

The layout is one of extreme formality. The site is a perfect square and within it *viali* run diagonally to the centre of each side forming a second square. This in turn contains a circular path surrounding a central fountain. Here one will find the most charming feature of this garden: the four little frescoed pavilions for public entertainments. The paths around the perimeter and the internal circle have been planted with elm and poplar, while the internal paths are made from *berceaux* of bitter orange. There is a receipt in the archives for 6000 citrus trees

and 980 poplars and elms. When Goethe saw it he described it, unfinished as it was, as 'the most beautiful place in the world. Exotic plants, citrus, pergolas, oleanders covered in thousands of flowers. Exotic trees … pools containing silver and gold fish … not Nature but a series of paintings'. At the far end of the central avenue is a pool with Marabitti's statue of the 'Spirit of Palermo'. Beyond this a large gate leads into the Botanic Gardens, though this is not normally open.

NEAREST MAJOR TOWN Palermo

MAIN FEATURES nineteenth-century English landscape garden, fine collection of specimen palms, baobabs, and so on.

PRE-BOOKING no

OWNER Fondazione Whitaker

ADDRESS Via Dante 167, I-90141 Palermo

LOCATION west of the city centre

OPEN Monday to Friday, 9.00–13.30

ADMISSION L5000

WHEELCHAIRS yes

REFRESHMENTS no

LAVATORIES yes

As Spain and Portugal had (and have) their great wine-exporting English dynasties, so too did Sicily. The wine in this case was Marsala, and the most successful of the families involved in this profitable trade was the Whitakers. Their business began in the 1830s and by 1850 they were well established in Palermo, where during the next half-century they would build three major villas. The first two to be built, Villa Sofia and Villa Sperlinga, have long since changed hands and have lost their gardens to the city's relentless expansion. The third, Villa Malfitano, is a remarkable survivor.

It was built in 1886 by Joseph Whitaker (known as 'Pip'), the second generation of the family to live in Sicily. He chose to build in an area known as 'Olivuzza' on the edge of the city, a place favoured by Sicilian nobility since the eighteenth century for its open views of the sea and mountains. The garden was planned by Emil Kunzmann (who had been head gardener to Pip's father at Villa Sofia) and laid out in the c. 4 hectares surrounding the villa in 1889. Sadly no records survive of plant purchases but it is likely that many plants came from the Orto Botanico in Palermo itself (page 369). Jean O'Neill (see Bibliography) wondered whether the Whitaker's trading fleet might not

have returned from Brazil or Australia with holds crammed with exotic plants.

Pip died in 1936. After the Second World War his daughter Delia made it her life's work to repair the war-damaged garden and to maintain it as her father had done. Before her death in 1970 she established the Fondazione Whitaker and left Villa Malfitano in its hands as a centre for archaeological research.

The garden is entered from Via Dante. The site is roughly rectangular with the villa at the centre. The drive divides around a palm-filled island and rejoins before the southern façade of the villa. This section of the garden contains many of the most spectacular tropical and sub-tropical plants; groves of enormous *Cycas revoluta* (sago palm) and *Chamaerops humilis* (fan palm). *Yucca elephantipes* has reached the same size here as in its native Mexico. Papyrus thrives in the lake below clumps of the black bamboo (*Phyllostachys nigra*).

Among the many varieties of fig grown here one will find a colossal *Ficus magnolioides* (Australian banyan, or pagoda tree) planted by Pip in 1888. When measured in the 1970s it was found to have a span of almost 43 metres. The formal gardens lie on the eastern side of the house. A *Wisteria sinensis* covers most of this side of the building together with a tangle of Banksian rose and the climber 'Marechal Niel'. From the shade one can look out over the complex spiral pattern of paths and parterres around the central fountain filled with the huge leaves of *Colocasia antiquorum*.

As the city expanded to cover the Olivuzzo so the planting was adjusted to provide shelter and privacy. This is mainly given by lavish use of cedar and *Ficus rubiginosa* or *Ficus benjamina*, the weeping fig, which now give height and shade to the garden. Although sadly run down, it is still worth seeing as an example of a completely unaltered nineteenth-century planting. Unweeded paths, crumbling grottoes and the like detract only a little from the pleasure of walking among so many surviving plants splendid in their maturity.

NEAREST MAJOR TOWN Palermo
MAIN FEATURES eighteenth-century botanic garden, one of the finest in Europe
PRE-BOOKING no
OWNER Università di Palermo
ADDRESS Via Lincoln, 1-90133 Palermo; tel.: +39 (0)91 6161493; fax.: (0)91 6176089

LOCATION beside Villa Giulia (page 363), a 5-minute walk from the central railway station
OPEN Monday to Friday, 9.00–17.00; Saturday and Sunday, 9.00–13.00; closed public holidays
ADMISSION free
WHEELCHAIRS yes
REFRESHMENTS no
LAVATORIES no

The earliest Sicilian botanical garden was established in 1638. By the middle of the following century a number of private botanical collections were flourishing in and around Palermo. In 1779 a Chair of Botany was established at the university and a garden was founded at Porta Carini. However, it soon became evident that it was inadequate for the purposes of teaching. As no further ground was available at this site it was decided to establish a new garden. Ground adjoining Villa Giulia was set aside for the purpose and work began in 1789. Costs were met by donations from the municipality, the Church, the royal family and other wealthy patrons. Both garden and buildings were predominantly the work of two men, Salvatore Attinelli and the French architect Leon Dufourny. Work was completed in 1795. The last major expansion of the garden took place in 1892.

The garden has often been under threat. During the anti-Bourbon uprising of 1820, 10,000 royalist troops took over the grounds and were besieged there for 11 days, destroying among other things 18,000 plant pots. Vincenzo Tineo, the director at that time, managed to

restore the garden in seven years. Evidence of the garden's importance as an intellectual centre is revealed by the subsequent Bourbon hostility to it. The royal family managed to prevent any further expansion of the garden, and no more land was bought until after the fall of the regime in 1860.

More recently, in 1946, it was proposed to run a main road straight through the centre of the garden. The plan was defeated after a 10-year campaign by the then director, Francesco Bruno (helped, so it is said, by the gardeners who in one night moved the historic ruins of a fifteenth-century church from a corner of the garden and rebuilt them on the route of the proposed road).

The original garden consisted of the four *quartini* where plants were grouped according to the then newly introduced Linnaean system of classification. It is entered through the Gymnasium from the Via Lincoln. This and the flanking buildings (the Tepidarium and Calidarium) all belong to the original plan. Over the years the original systematised planting has become confused. From the centre of the *quartini* a palm-lined avenue runs left to the original entrance to Villa Giulia, now shut. Following the avenue to the right leads to Viale Vincenzo Tineo, lined with a fine collection of *Quercus*. The soap tree, *Sapindus mukorossii*, will also be found here; the fruits will produce a lather if rubbed with wet hands. Beyond the avenue stands the oldest of the greenhouses built in England in 1790 for 24,000 ducats for the Austrian Emperor, who then decided not to take it. The builder then sold it to the Queen of the Two Sicilies originally for use in the gardens at Caserta (page 347), though it was eventually presented to the Orto Botanico in 1799. It was then dismantled and stored till 1823 when the money was found to erect it.

At the far end of the central avenue, opposite the Gymnasium, is the Aquarium. Not a home for tropical fish, this is a magnificent circular pool of three concentric rings divided into 24 separate compartments. They are filled with many species of waterlily, lotus, and so on. Around the pool grow several species of bamboo (*Vulgaris*, the huge *macroculmis*, *spinosa* and *gracilis*). Beyond it grows the colossal *Ficus magnolioides*, or pagoda tree. This is a spectacularly beautiful spot and should not be missed.

NEAREST MAJOR TOWN Catania

MAIN FEATURES late nineteenth-century English garden with twentieth-century alterations made around a thirteenth-century abbey, once owned by Admiral Lord Nelson

PRE-BOOKING no

OWNER Comune di Bronte

ADDRESS 1-95030 Maniace Bronte; tel.: +39 (0)95 690018

LOCATION Maniace is off the ss120 Randazzo to Cesaro road. The *castello* is on the left immediately before the bridge into Maniace (there is no sign at the gate at the time of writing). The *castello* is signposted from the main road, also from the centre of Bronte

OPEN dawn to dusk. The *castello* is currently being restored. To visit, contact the Comune; tel.: (0)95 7723040

ADMISSION free

WHEELCHAIRS no

REFRESHMENTS no

LAVATORIES no

Little is known of the early history of this thirteenth-century monastery. By 1799 the then ruined building and c. 12,000 hectares of the surrounding countryside came into the possession of Admiral Lord Nelson. It was given to him (together with the Dukedom of Bronte) by the Bourbon King Ferdinand of the Two Sicilies as a reward for Nelson's daring rescue of the royal family from the advancing French army. Nelson never visited the estate, which was perhaps as well. To offer, in return for one's life, a meaningless title and a bandit-ridden stretch of uninhabitable ground on the side of a volcano was an entirely typical Bourbon gesture.

It was to be 70 years before any member of the family paid more than a fleeting visit to Maniace. In 1873 Viscount Bridport sent his fourth son Alec Hood to Sicily, and it was he who first paid any attention to the estate. He devoted the greater part of his life to modernising

it, including restoring the *castello* and from 1876 laying out a garden. During the 1970s the garden was substantially replanted by Vernon Russell-Smith. In 1981 what remained of the estate and castello was sold to the Comune.

The original approach was by way of an avenue that ran through the woods opposite the house. This is now overgrown, and the wood is filled with weirdly inappropriate contemporary sculptures. The garden is entered through the house. It is highly formal in an English way, laid out on a flat rectangular site of about 0.2 hectare, surrounded by walls.

A central path leads between box-edged parterres under the remains of a pergola to a small ornamental pool. Further box-edged enclosures contain the magnificent palms and magnolias which are now all that remain of the original Victorian planting. There are many contemporary accounts of the garden at its peak, of the parterres filled with roses and bedding plants, but above all of the wild garden that lay along the bank of the river. This was reached through the gate at the far end of the formal garden. It is currently inaccessible but has in any case returned to wilderness. At its peak it must have been breathtaking, planted by Hood with shrubs and bulbs to flower spectacularly in the spring.

In the 1970s the parterres nearest the house were removed and the plantings in the rest renewed. A collection of old roses is clustered around the bases of the palms. Elsewhere new beds were created and planted, according to Charles Quest-Ritson, to suggest the fantasy gardens found in the Pre-Raphaelite paintings of Dante Gabriel Rossetti.

The place is currently in a sad state. None of the replanting of 20 years ago survives. Even the roses, which will last untended for generations, have completely vanished. However, thanks to Hood's trees and hedges the garden does not look completely unfurnished. The castello is under restoration, and if the will and the money are there it should not be an enormous task to restore at least the formal area.

NEAREST MAJOR TOWN Taormina
MAIN FEATURES nineteenth-century Anglo-Italian garden, unusual follies, magnificent views
PRE-BOOKING no
OWNER Comune di Taormina
ADDRESS Via Roma, 1-98039 Taormina
LOCATION on the southern edge of town, a few minutes walk from the centre
OPEN dawn to dusk
ADMISSION free
WHEELCHAIRS yes (not to bar or lavatories)
REFRESHMENTS yes
LAVATORIES yes (see above)

The tide of northern visitors that swept across Europe during the nineteenth century in search of sunshine and culture reached perhaps its most southerly point at Taormina on the eastern coast of Sicily. By 1890 the little town had become a magnet for tourists – not surprisingly, for it is undeniably one of the world's great beauty spots. A number of visitors settled here, among them Florence Trevelyan, from a well-known Northumbrian family. An only child and reasonably well-off through the early death of her parents, she married the local doctor, Salvatore Cacciola. She bought a stretch of land just outside the wall of the town above a steep cliff overlooking the sea and made a garden there, which she continued to elaborate until her early death in 1907 at the age of 55. After her husband's death the garden passed through various hands until in 1923 it was given to the Comune.

The garden is laid out on three levels on a long strip of land that meanders along the edge of a cliff. On entering, one is at the start of a long avenue lined with olives, each bearing a small placard to the memory of a soldier fallen in one or other of the world wars. It is almost impossible to resist turning right to the long balustraded walk where the mountainside falls about 210 metres to the sea and the view

sicily (sicilia)

extends 40 kilometres to Catania and snow-capped Mount Etna. Unlike many other gardens in Italy, the view does not come as a surprise; indeed there is nowhere in Taormina where one is unaware of its spectacular position. Florence achieved her surprises in a quite different way. Even before the garden was laid out she started work on a most remarkable collection of buildings, dotted apparently at random around the site. Two took their form from the remains of existing buildings, but the rest are free-standing and completely *sui generis*. They were built out of any material that came to hand – terracotta pipes and tiles, brick, stone, tree trunks and branches, wrought-iron – to give an incredible variety of effects. The tallest of these constructions, 'The Beehives', is five stories high. It stands at the far end of the garden in a grove of maritime pines, overlooking a collection of 'standing stones' and a small aviary. Nearby a group of inscribed stones commemorates the family dogs, loved by Florence but not by the inhabitants of Taormina, to judge by their sad ends: 'Dear Fanny, Faithful Friend & Companion, Poisoned 27 July 1899'. Elsewhere dense hedges of bougainvillaea line the walks and enclose the beds.

The Comune di Taormina is to be praised for maintaining these gardens with such care and attention to detail. Florence would find little to complain about today, except perhaps for the notice at the gate: 'Vietato Introdurre Cani'.

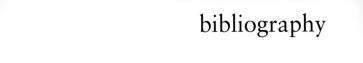
bibliography

James Ackerman, *The Villa: Form and Ideology of Country Houses*, Thames & Hudson, 1990

Harold Acton, *Tuscan Villas*, Thames & Hudson, 1973

Giuseppe Chigiotti, 'The design and realization of the park of the Royal Palace at Caserta by Luigi and Carlo Vanvitelli', *Journal of Garden History*, v/2 (1985), pp. 184–206

Ethne Clarke, 'A biography of Cecil Ross Pinsent, 1884–1963', *Garden History*, XXVI/2 (1998), 176–91

David R Coffin, *Gardens and Gardening in Papal Rome*, Princeton University Press, 1992

David R Coffin, *The Villa d'Este at Tivoli*, Princeton University Press, 1960

David R Coffin, *The Villa in the Life of Renaissance Rome*, Princeton University Press, 1979

Maris A Conelli, 'Boboil Gardens: fountains and propaganda in six-teenth-century Florence', *Studies in the History of Gardens and Designed Landscapes* [formerly *Journal of Garden History*], XVIII/4 (1998), 300–16

Margaretta J Darnall and Mark S Weil, 'Il Sacro Bosco di Bomarzo: its 16th-century literary and antiquarian context', *Journal of Garden History*, IV/1 (1984), pp. 1–94

Christopher Hibbert, *The Rise and Fall of the House of Medici*, Penguin, 1979

John Dixon Hunt, *Garden and Grove: The Italian Garden in the English Imagination 1600–1750*, revised, University of Pennsylvania Press, 1996

John Dixon Hunt (ed.), *The Italian Garden: Art, Design and Culture*, Cambridge University Press, 1996

John Dixon Hunt, 'The garden in the city of Venice: epitome of state and site', *Studies in the History of Gardens and Designed Landscapes* [formerly *Journal of Garden History*], XIX/1 (1999), 46–61

John Ingamells, *A Dictionary of British and Irish Travellers in Italy 1701–1800*, Yale University Press, 1997

Jeffrey A Jellicoe and S Jellicoe, *The Oxford Companion to Gardens*, Oxford University Press, 1986

Claudia Lazzaro, *The Italian Renaissance Garden: From the Conventions of Planting Design and Ornament to the Grand Gardens of Sixteenth-century Central Italy*, Yale University Press, 1990

Alvide Lees-Milne, 'Ninfa: a garden in the ruins of a town', *Hortus*, V (1988), pp. 40–9

C Lodari Carola, *Villa San Remigio a Pallanza, I Quaderni*, vol. 1, Museo del Paesaggio, Verbania

Roberto Lucofero and Luigi Berliocchi, *Guida ai Giardini Perduti di Roma/Vanished Gardens of Rome: A Guide Book*, exhibition catalogue, Academia Italiana/Di Baio, 1995

Georgina Masson, *Italian Gardens*, Thames & Hudson, 1961

Jean O'Neill, *Country Life*, April 1984

E M Phillips and E T Bolton, *The Gardens of Italy*, London, 1919

Pierre de la Ruffiniere du Prey, *The Villas of Pliny: From Antiquity to Posterity*, Chicago, 1994

Charles Quest-Ritson, *The English Garden Abroad*, Viking, 1992

Paul van der Ree, Gerrit Smienk and Clemens Steenbergen, *Italian Villas and Gardens*, 2nd edn, Prestel, 1993

Regione del Veneto, *Il Giardino Veneto*, Electa, 1988

Vincent Shacklock and David Mason, 'Villa Le Balze, Fiesole, Florence: a broad assessment of "A modern garden in the Italian style"',

Journal of Garden History, XV/3 (1995), pp. 179–87

J C Shepherd and Jeffrey A Jellicoe, *Italian Gardens of the Renaissance*, London, 1925

Alessandro Tagliolini, *Storia del giardino italiano*, Usher, 1988

Else M Terwen-Dionisius, 'Date and design of the botanical garden in Padua', *Journal of Garden History*, XIV/4 (1994), pp. 213–35.

H Inigo Triggs, *The Art of Garden Design In Italy*, London, 1906

M A Visentina, 'La grotta nel cinquecento veneto: il Giardino Giusti di Verona', *Arte Veneta Annata*, XXXIX

Edith Wharton, *Italian Villas and their Gardens*, New York, 1904

glossary

AUTOMATA hydraulically powered human or animal figures designed to move, spout water or play musical instruments

BERCEAU (pl. BERCEAUX) an arched pergola or tunnel supporting climbing plants such as the vine

BOSCO (pl. BOSCHI) a wooded area enclosed in a garden that owes its origins to the 'sacred grove' of both the Greeks and Romans, and which provided the essential touch of wildness in the otherwise ordered world of the garden

CARYATID sculptured female figure used as a supporting column

CASINO a small house

GIARDINO ALL'ITALIANA garden in the Italian style, usually a formal arrangement of box parterres, often arranged around a fountain

GIARDINO SEGRETO a secret garden, originally a small area enclosed for privacy but later a major feature of many gardens

GIOCHI D'ACQUA 'water games'; concealed sprays designed to surprise the visitor

HERM a garden ornament/statue of a three-quarter-length figure on a pedestal

LIMONAIA a shelter for overwintering potted citrus trees, sometimes referred to as a '*stanzone*'

MANÈGE an open space for riding practise

NYMPHAEUM in classical gardens a shrine or grotto with fountains dedicated to the nymphs

PALAZZINA a small villa

PARTERRE a flowerbed laid out in a regular manner

PARTERRE DE BRODERIE a bed laid out with an elaborate flowing pattern often formed from clipped box (broderie/embroidery)

PESCHIERA a fishpool

PIANO NOBILE the principal floor of a house, usually on the first floor

PUTTO (pl. PUTTI) cupid or cherub

QUINCUNX a grove of trees planted in regular arrangements of fives; typically, one at each corner of a square and one in the centre

RAGNAIA (pl. RAGNAIE) a bird snare made of nets covered in bird lime and stretched between the branches of trees

ROCAILLE elaborate decoration of rock-like forms, shells and scrolls

SPUGNE rough texturing of grotto walls in imitation of coral

TAPIS VERT a (usually rectangular) stretch of grass

TERM a tapering pedestal bearing a bust and used as boundary markers in the ancient world

biographies

ALEOTTI, Giovanni Battista (1546–1636) Architect from Parma; worked in Parma and Ferrara

ALESSI, Galeazzo (1512–72) Leading Genoese architect, born in Perugia and trained in Rome, where he was influenced by Michelangelo, and Milan

ALGARDI, Alessandro (1595–1654) Sculptor, decorator, architect. Born and trained in Bologna; active in Venice, Mantua, Rome and Naples

AMMANATI, Bartolommeo (1511–92) Architect and sculptor influenced by Michelangelo and Jacopo Sansovino. Born in Florence and trained by Bandinelli; worked in Venice, Padua, Rome and Florence

BANDINELLI, Baccio (1493–1560) Florentine painter and sculptor much influenced by Michelangelo

BERNINI, Pietro (1562–1629) Florentine sculptor. Worked in Naples and Rome. Father of the architect and sculptor Gianlorenzo Bernini

BONAZZA, Giovanni (active 1695–1730) Venetian sculptor

BORROMINI, Francesco (1559–1667) Brilliantly original if eccentric baroque architect. Born in Lombardy; worked principally in Rome

BRAMANTE, Donato (1444–1514) One of the greatest Renaissance architects. Influenced by Leonardo da Vinci. Born in Urbino; worked principally in Rome

BUONTALENTI, Bernado (1531–1608) Mannerist architect, sculptor and painter working in Tuscany

CASSETTI, Giacomo (1682–1757) Venetian sculptor; trained under Grazio Marinali

CERRATO, Domenico (1715–92) Architect from Vicenza; worked mainly in Padua

COLLINO, Filippo (1737–?) Piedmontese sculptor working for the House of Savoy

COLLINO, Ignazio (1724–93) Piedmontese sculptor working for the House of Savoy

DAL POZZO, Girolamo (1718–1800) Veronese architect

DA UDINE, Giovanni (1487–1564) Decorative artist; studied under Raphael

FONTANA, Carlo (1634–1714) Architect working mainly in Rome. Trained under Bernini, among others

FONTANA, Giovanni (1540–1614) Hydraulic engineer; worked mainly in and around Rome

FRIGIMELICA, Girolamo (1653–1732) Venetian architect

GENGA, Girolamo (1476–1551) Painter and architect from Urbino. Influenced by Raphael

GIAMBOLOGNA (Giovanni Bologna or Jean Boulogne) (1529–1608) Flemish-born Mannerist architect and sculptor. Trained in Antwerp, worked mainly in Florence

LE NÔTRE, André (1613–1700) French gardener; best-known work at Versailles and Vaux-le-Vicomte; also worked in England

LIGORIO, Pirro (c. 1510–83) Painter, architect and archaeologist. Born in Naples; worked mostly in Rome

MADERNO, Carlo (c. 1556–1629) Architect; born in Lombardy, worked in Rome

MARCHIONNI, Carlo (1702–86) Roman architect

MARCHIORI, Giovanni (1696–1778) Sculptor working in Venice

MARINALI, Orazio (1643–1720) Venetian Baroque sculptor

MICHELOZZI, Michelozzo di Bartolommeo (1396–1472) Florentine architect, sculptor and decorator. Worked in Florence for Cosimo the Elder and in Milan

MUTTONI, Francesco (?–1748) Venetian architect

PERUZZI, Baldassare (1481–1536) Sienese architect and painter; worked mostly in Rome with Bramante and Raphael

PINSENT, Cecil R (1884–1964) English architect and landscape designer. Worked in England, Italy and Yugoslavia

PORTA, Giacomo della (c. 1533–1602) Lombard Mannerist architect working mainly in Rome; follower of Michelangelo

RAINALDI, Girolamo (1570–1655) Roman architect

RAPHAEL (Raffaello Sanzio) (1483–1520) Painter and architect, born in Urbino. From 1508 worked in Rome. Perhaps the greatest Renaissance artist in the classical style

RIPAMONTE, Riccardo (1849–1930) Milanese sculptor

ROMANO, Giulio (1499–1546) Mannerist architect and painter; worked mostly in Mantua and Rome. Assistant to Raphael; also influenced by Michelangelo

ROSSETTI, Biagio (c. 1447–1516) Born in Bologna. Town-planner and architect for the Ferrarese court

SANGALLO, Antonio da (the Younger) (1483–1546) Roman architect. Born in Florence; trained under Bramante and Peruzzi, assistant to Raphael

SCAMOZZI, Vincenzo (1552–1616) Venetian architect, born in Vicenza; follower of Andrea Palladio

TACCA, Pietro (1577–1640) Florentine sculptor and pupil of Giambologna; worked in Florence and Livorno

TIBALDI, Pellegrino (Il Pellegrini) (1527–96) Lombard architect and painter. Worked in Rome, Milan and Spain

TIRALI, Andrea (1660–37) Venetian Baroque architect and sculptor

TRIBOLO (pseudonym for Niccolo Pericoli) (1485–1550) Florentine sculptor and engineer

VALVASSORI, Gabriele (1683–1750) Roman architect

VANSANZIO, Giovanni van Santen (?–1622) Known as Il Fiammingo. Flemish architect working in Rome

VANVITELLI, Luigi (1700–73) Neapolitan architect; worked in Rome, Naples and Ancona

VIGNOLA, Giacomo Barozzi da (1507–73) Leading Roman architect. Born near Moderna, studied at Bologna; worked with Ammanati and Giorgio Vasari. Wrote the highly influential *Regole delle cinque ordini* (1562)

VITTORIA, Alessandro (1525–1608) Venetian sculptor. Influenced by da Udine

index

italian gardens: a guide

italian gardens: a guide